# U.S.
# Territories

# U.S. Territories

*Sylvia McNair*

Children's Press®
A Division of Grolier Publishing
New York   London   Hong Kong   Sydney
Danbury, Connecticut

Frontispiece: Sunset on St. John, U.S. Virgin Islands

Front cover: A house in Charlotte Amalie, capital of the Virgin Islands

Back cover: Magens Bay on the north coast of St. Thomas Island

Consultant: Shirley Lincoln, Virgin Islands Division of Libraries, Archives and Museums

*Please note: All statistics are as up-to-date as possible at the time of publication.*

Visit Children's Press on the Internet at http://publishing.grolier.com

Book production by Editorial Directions, Inc.

Library of Congress Cataloging-in-Publication Data

McNair, Sylvia.
    U.S. Territorities / Sylvia McNair.
        p. cm. — (America the beautiful. Second series)
    Includes bibliographical references (p. ) and index.
    Summary: Describes the geography, plants and animals, history, economy, language,
religions, culture, sports and arts, and people of the various United States territories.
    ISBN 0-516-21607-4
    1. United States—Territories and possessions—Juvenile literature. 2. United States—
Insular possessions—Juvenile literature. [1. United States—Territories and possession. 2.
United States—Insular possessions.] I. Title. II. Series.
F965 .M38 2001
973—dc21
                                                                            00-026194
                                                                               CIP
                                                                               AC

## Acknowledgments

The author is grateful to the U.S. Virgin Islands Department of Tourism and the Martin Public Relations Agency for help in researching this book. Thanks particularly to Susanna Riddle, Amy Adkinson, Talia Woodard, and Yolanda Arroyo. Thanks also to Kathy O'Neil for her hospitality, Luana Wheatley for reading the manuscript and making helpful suggestions, and Anna Idol for her meticulous copyediting.

A village in
American Samoa

St. John

Waterfall in Guam

# Contents

Sea lion

Pago Pago

Picking coconuts

A Virgin Islander

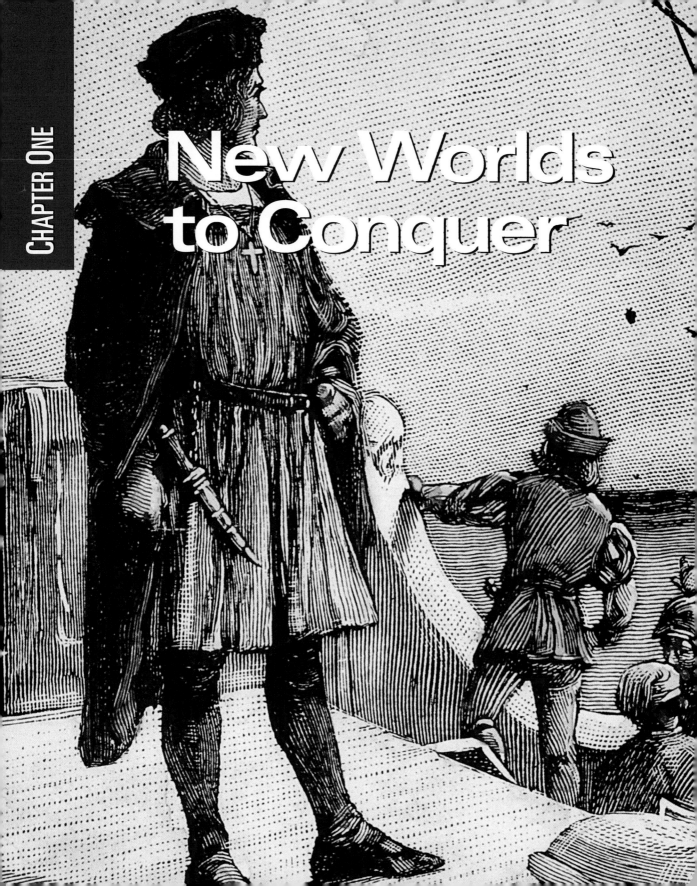

# CHAPTER ONE

# New Worlds to Conquer

**Ferdinand Magellan's fleet finding a passage to the Pacific**

We have new worlds to conquer! Imagine how the kings and queens and wealthy merchants felt when they heard about the voyages of Christopher Columbus, Vasco da Gama, John Cabot, Vasco Nuñez de Balboa, and Ferdinand Magellan. The news spread fast, mostly by word of mouth. Gutenberg's printing press was only recently invented. Radio and television would not be invented for several hundred years, but news got around anyway.

Traders from Europe sailed to the islands known as the Indies in search of silks, spices, and other luxury goods. Pirates followed them on the high seas, intent on taking these valuables away from them. Explorers led expeditions to find and chart lands not yet on any maps. Gradually, people in different parts of the world were learning about one another.

Columbus, sailing for the Spanish royals, found some islands on the other side of the Atlantic Ocean. Cabot, exploring for the English, spotted a large landmass far north of where Columbus landed. Da Gama, a Portuguese explorer, made his way from Lisbon, Portugal, to the Far East by sailing around the southern tip of Africa. Balboa, a Spanish conquistador in what is now Central America, spotted a vast ocean to the west, which he called the South Sea. Shortly after that, Captain Ferdinand Magellan of

**Opposite: Christopher Columbus watching for land**

Portugal, perhaps the greatest explorer of them all, led an expedition that sailed all the way around the world. He renamed Balboa's discovery the Pacific Ocean.

"Explorers are finding places on Earth that we didn't know existed," European leaders must have thought. "We can send people out to settle these places and build up new colonies." New colonies were important. They meant new markets, possibly gold and other precious minerals, and at least, new sources of taxes.

All these world-changing explorations took place between 1492 and 1521, a period of less than thirty years. But they set off a scramble that continued for nearly 400 years after that. European nations—Great Britain, Spain, France, the Netherlands, Portugal, and others—struggled to grab land and set up colonies in the Americas, Africa, Asia, and the islands of the world. The Europeans competed with one another for both economic and political power and used military force when necessary.

In 1776, settlers in a group of colonies located along the North American shore of the Atlantic Ocean decided they were tired of being dominated by a European power. They joined together to declare their independence from Great Britain. They won their independence in a revolution and called their new country the United States of America.

At first, the young United States was interested only in expanding its territory across North America, not in overseas conquests. The citizens didn't think they wanted to build an empire. After all, they had fought to separate themselves from the British Empire. But world events and changing circumstances over the next 200 years brought certain other parts of the world into the U.S. family.

Today, the United States includes fifty states and Washington, D.C., three territories, two closely allied commonwealths, and dozens of islands around the world.

The territories and commonwealths are all island regions. The Virgin Islands of the United States and the Commonwealth of Puerto Rico are in the Caribbean Sea. The Commonwealth of the Northern Marianas, the Territory of American Samoa, and the Territory of Guam are all in the western part of the Pacific Ocean. Their languages, cultures, ethnic backgrounds, and religions differ greatly. Some cities on the U.S. mainland have more people than all these islands combined, but the American flag flies over each of them.

A village in
American Samoa

# CHAPTER TWO

# From Sea to Sea

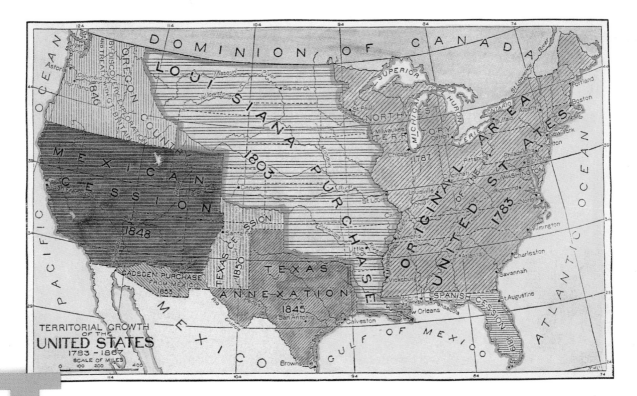

The territorial growth
of the United States
from 1783 to 1867

The Revolutionary War (1775–1783) was over, and the colonies had won. Great Britain signed the Treaty of Paris in 1783, recognizing the independence of a new nation, the United States of America.

Britain gave up its claims to the territory between the Atlantic Ocean and the Mississippi River. The Spanish held the land in the south that is now Florida. The northern border of the United States with Canada was not clearly defined until 1818.

Individual colonies along the Atlantic Coast claimed part of the lands that stretched west to the Mississippi. Some of these claims were in dispute. During the debates over the U.S. Constitution, all the colonies agreed to give their western lands to the federal government.

Opposite: Early American settlers in the southern Appalachians

From Sea to Sea **13**

## The Northwest Ordinance

Thirteen states—the thirteen former British colonies—established the Constitution of the United States in 1787. During its first century as a nation, the United States managed to gain control of a great deal of land. It bought large tracts, acquired others through negotiations and treaties, and took over still more as the result of military victories.

In 1787, the U.S. Congress passed the Northwest Ordinance. This important law established the Northwest Territory, which consisted of all the land between the original states and the Mississippi River, as far south as the Ohio River. Five states—Ohio, Indiana, Illinois, Michigan, Wisconsin—and part of Minnesota were eventually created out of the Northwest Territory.

The ordinance also provided a model for setting up new, self-governing states. First, Congress would appoint a governor, a secretary, and three judges to administer a territory. The government would survey the land and establish land offices. Settlers could then buy parcels of land to live on. Money from these sales would be used to build public schools and other facilities.

Then, when a territory had grown in population to at least 5,000 adult males, its people could elect a legislature and send a nonvoting representative to Congress. When the total population reached at least 60,000, the territory could apply for statehood—with the right to adopt a state constitution and elect its own state government.

The Northwest Ordinance contained other important provisions, too. No one born in the territory could be forced into

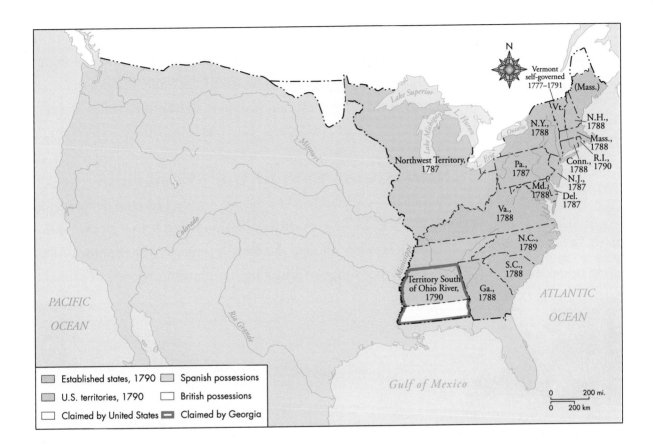

Map legend:
- Established states, 1790
- U.S. territories, 1790
- Claimed by United States
- Spanish possessions
- British possessions
- Claimed by Georgia

Map labels:
Vermont self-governed 1777–1791, (Mass.), N.H., 1788, N.Y., 1788, Mass., 1788, Vt., R.I., 1790, Conn., 1788, Northwest Territory, 1787, Pa., 1787, N.J., 1787, Md., 1788, Del., 1787, Va., 1788, N.C., 1789, Territory South of Ohio River, 1790, S.C., 1788, Ga., 1788, PACIFIC OCEAN, ATLANTIC OCEAN, Gulf of Mexico, Lake Superior, L. Huron, Erie, Ontario, Missouri, Colorado, Rio Grande, Mississippi

0 200 mi.
0 200 km

slavery. The ordinance also guaranteed trial by jury, freedom of religion, and fair treatment of Native Americans. In addition, it promoted public education. Unfortunately, the government did not always live up to its promises, especially to Native Americans and African slaves.

The U.S. Constitution based representation in the House of Representatives on the number of people in each state. So the government needed to know how many people lived in its states and territories. To carry this out, a count of the population was nec-

**The United States in 1790**

essary. According to the Constitution, a count of the population of each state and territory would be made every ten years. This count is called a census. The 1790 Census of the United States reported slightly fewer than 4 million people in the thirteen states and territories.

## New States East of the Mississippi

Two states—Vermont and Kentucky—were admitted to the Union in 1791 and 1792, respectively. Vermont had set up its own independent republic during the Revolutionary War. Kentucky had originally been part of Virginia, but chose to become a separate

**Settlers making their way through the new state of Vermont.**

state. Maine was part of Massachusetts until 1820, when it broke away and formed its own state government.

Congress passed another ordinance in 1790 to establish the Territory South of the Ohio River. The states of Tennessee, Mississippi, and Alabama were created from this territory.

The region that would later become Florida still belonged to Spain. The rest of the land east of the Mississippi River was rapidly becoming absorbed into the United States.

Although the Industrial Revolution was starting in this country, most Americans depended on the land for a living. A few frontiersmen survived by hunting and fishing, but most people lived on farms. Many of them, however, had large families, and their farms were not big enough to support all their children and grandchildren. As a result, the descendants began to move west in search of farmland. Northeasterners, for the most part, moved west into the Northwest Territory, while southerners went to the Territory South of the Ohio River.

President Thomas Jefferson

## The Louisiana Purchase

President Thomas Jefferson became president of the United States in 1801. Only eighteen years had passed since the Revolutionary War, but the country already had sixteen states—the original thirteen plus Vermont, Kentucky, and Tennessee—and two large territories. The Mississippi River was still the nation's western boundary, however.

Meanwhile, European nations, especially France, Great Britain, and Spain, had been struggling throughout the 1700s to gain and keep colonies in the Americas.

France had claimed a vast section of land west of the Mississippi River in 1682. Most of it was unexplored, and only a few Europeans had settled there. France called the region Louisiana, after their king, Louis XIV. It covered more than 828,000 square miles (2,144,520 square kilometers) of land between the Mississippi and the Rocky Mountains. In 1762, France ceded, or granted, Louisiana to Spain.

New Orleans, Louisiana, was a thriving Spanish port. Americans regularly used the city for trade and transportation along the Mississippi River. Then, in 1802, the Spanish cut off American shipping privileges. Two years earlier, Spain had secretly agreed to transfer Louisiana back to France, but France did not take possession.

President Jefferson decided to send two representatives to France to negotiate a purchase of the city of New Orleans. To their great surprise, the representatives found that Napoléon Bonaparte, ruler of France, had lost his desire to build an empire in the Western Hemisphere. He offered to sell the Louisiana Territory for about $15 million. Jefferson's Louisiana Purchase is considered as one of the greatest land bargains ever made.

**Napoléon Bonaparte was ruler of France when the United States bought the Louisiana Territory.**

With the Louisiana Purchase on December 20, 1803, the size of the United States instantly doubled. Fifteen of today's fifty U.S. states were originally part of the Louisiana Territory. In addition, the United States gained control of the mighty Mississippi River, the main transportation artery in the center of the country.

Jefferson had dreams of building a great nation that would stretch across the continent. He wanted to prevent European nations from colonizing land bordering the United States. He encouraged both settlers and Native Americans to move west and establish new settlements.

**The United States in 1830**

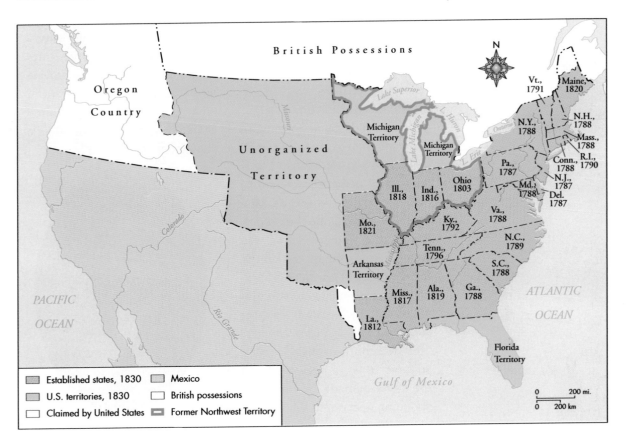

Legend:
- Established states, 1830
- U.S. territories, 1830
- Claimed by United States
- Mexico
- British possessions
- Former Northwest Territory

## The Lewis and Clark Expedition

In May 1804, Captain Lewis and his associate, William Clark (below), set out on the Lewis and Clark Expedition. It was one of the most important endeavors in U.S. history. The journey from St. Louis, Missouri, to the mouth of the Columbia River in Oregon and back again took two years and four months. All members of the group were instructed to keep journals and write down descriptions of everything they saw— plants, animals, people, and landforms. These journals provide an excellent historical record of what the northwestern United States was like before people changed it. ■

Even before the purchase of the Louisiana Territory was completed, President Thomas Jefferson had made plans to explore the lands west of the Mississippi. He had chosen Meriwether Lewis (above), his personal secretary, to lead an expedition up the Missouri River and along the Columbia to the Pacific Ocean. He wanted the explorers to find the most direct and practicable land-and-water passage across the continent. In addition, he instructed Lewis to judge whether "the Missouri country" could support "a large population, in the same manner as the corresponding tract on the Ohio."

## Other Spanish Lands

At the beginning of the 1800s, Spain still held present-day Florida and much of the land that is now Mexico and the southwestern United States. But Spanish control over Florida was weak. Native Americans clashed with American settlers near the Florida–Georgia border. In 1818, General Andrew Jackson (later president) invaded west Florida and prepared to take east Florida by force. In 1819, Spain yielded to the military pressure and signed over all of Florida to the United States.

The fall of the Alamo in Texas, 1836

The Mexicans were increasingly unhappy with Spanish rule, and an uprising that began in 1810 grew into a full-fledged revolution. Spain recognized Mexican independence eleven years later.

The United States and Mexico enjoyed friendly relations for a while, and Mexico allowed U.S. settlers to move into their lands. Soon there were more Americans than Mexicans in what is now Texas. The Americans revolted against Mexican rule in 1835. After several battles, the Texans formed their own government, the Republic of Texas. President Andrew

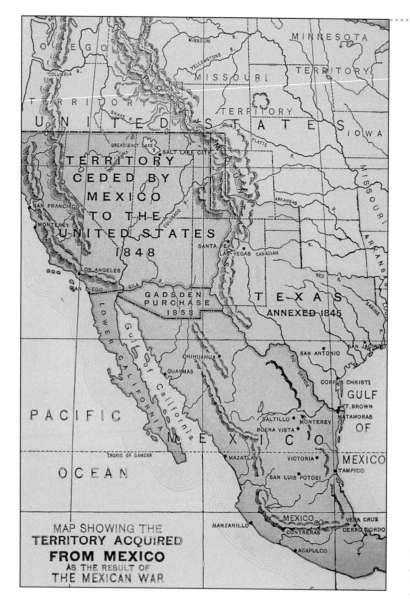

MAP SHOWING THE
**TERRITORY ACQUIRED**
**FROM MEXICO**
AS THE RESULT OF
THE MEXICAN WAR

**Land acquired from Mexico during the Mexican War, 1846–1848**

Jackson formally recognized it in 1837.

The Americans in Texas wanted to become a part of the United States. So, in 1845, the U.S. government annexed Texas.

The following year, the United States declared war on Mexico. In 1848, Mexico and the United States signed the Treaty of Guadalupe Hidalgo. Mexico sold its lands west of Texas to the United States for $15 million. More than 525,000 square miles (1,359,750 sq km) were added to the nation with this purchase. The territory included the present-day states of California, Nevada, Utah, most of Arizona, and parts of New Mexico, Colorado, and Wyoming.

## Treaties with Britain

While the United States was expanding into lands claimed by Spain, and later by Mexico, the nation was also in land disputes with Great Britain. One disagreement was settled in 1818. Britain

## Manifest Destiny

A New York newspaper editor, John Louis O'Sullivan, voiced the opinion of many U.S. citizens about the Mexican disputes. He wrote, in 1845, "Our manifest destiny [is] to overspread and to possess the whole of the continent which Providence had given us for the development of the great experiment of liberty and federated self-government entrusted to us."

Politicians and others in favor of expanding U.S. authority across the continent loved the words *manifest destiny*. It was the slogan they needed to justify grabbing land by any means.

Forty years later, an influential historian and philosopher named John Fiske gave a lecture titled "Manifest Destiny." He argued that the Anglo-Saxon people were destined to rule over less-gifted races by the logic of survival of the fittest. Many Americans bought into this philosophy. They claimed the superiority of the United States on racial, military, religious, moral, economic, and geographic grounds.

Fifty years after John Fiske's lecture, a German named Adolf Hitler was spouting a similar belief about a "superior race." ■

For a time, the Oregon Country was jointly owned by the United States and Great Britain.

gave up its claim to lands that are now Minnesota and the Dakotas. The agreement, known as the Red River Cession, fixed the northern border of U.S. lands at the forty-ninth parallel.

At the same time, the two countries agreed to joint occupation of the land known as the Oregon Country. This area consisted of the land between the western border of the Louisiana Purchase and the Pacific Ocean, north of the lands claimed by Spain. The joint occupation treaty expired in 1846, and Britain offered to grant the Oregon Country to the United States.

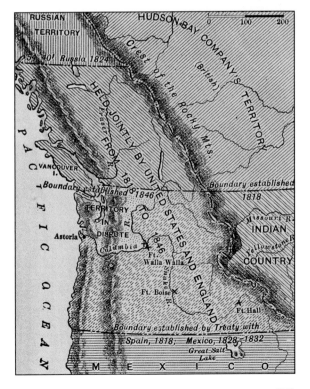

## The Gadsden Purchase

In 1853, the United States bought another parcel of land along the border with Mexico for $10 million. This piece, called the Gadsden Purchase, added another 29,640 square miles (76,768 sq km) to the country. Many people hoped the land would be used as the route for a new railroad. With the Gadsden Purchase, the borders of the United States became approximately the same as they are today.

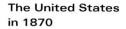

**The United States in 1870**

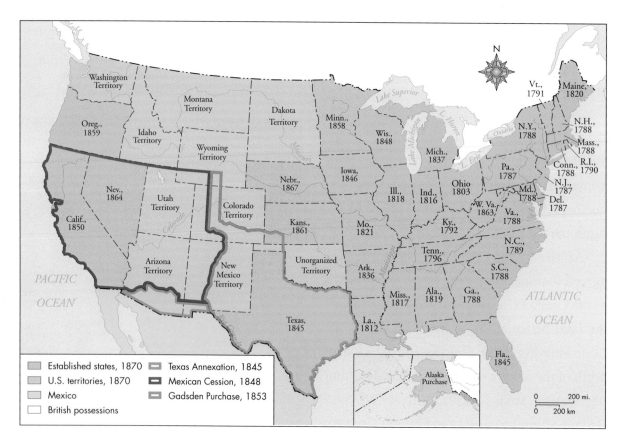

## The 1800s—A Century of Expansion

| Year | Number of States | U.S.Population |
|------|------------------|---------------|
| 1790 | 13 | 3,929,214 |
| 1800 | 16 | 5,308,483 |
| 1810 | 17 | 7,239,881 |
| 1820 | 22 | 9,638,453 |
| 1830 | 24 | 12,866,020 |
| 1840 | 26 | 17,069,453 |
| 1850 | 31 | 23,191,876 |
| 1860 | 33 | 31,443,321 |
| 1870 | 37 | 38,558,371 |
| 1880 | 38 | 50,155,783 |
| 1890 | 43 | 62,974,714 |
| 1900 | 45 | 75,994,575 |

## Westward Migrations

There was a lot of land out west. Some of it could be bought for as little as $1 or $2 an acre (0.4 hectare), and some was actually free to new settlers under certain conditions. The Louisiana Purchase had added many thousands of acres to the nation, and not many people were living on them. White settlers gave very little thought to the Native Americans and their rights.

So, the western migration, which had begun even before the Revolutionary War, continued. Waves of settlers rolled across the Appalachian Mountains, the Mississippi River, and the Great Plains toward the Rocky Mountains and the Pacific Ocean. As families established new villages and towns, pressure was growing to carve the land into more and more states.

Promises of land lured many settlers to the American West.

The history of that western migration is many-sided. It is a story of adventure, courage, hard work, and determination on the part of many ordinary people. Sadly, it is also a story of warfare and the exploitation of Native Americans. Lands were taken without payment, and treaties were broken.

In addition, it is a story of struggles to satisfy different interests. The United States was not totally united. There were strong regional feelings. Merchants and industrialists in the Northeast, plantation owners in the South, and small farmers in the Midwest all tried to protect their interests in national politics. Each new state sent new senators and representatives to Congress, threatening

Cutting sugarcane on a Southern plantation

the power of those already in the Union. The most intense—but not the only—disagreement was between the states that permitted slavery and those that did not.

Over time, the nation survived the disagreements—even a civil war—and continued to grow. Factories and railroad companies welcomed new settlers. Immigrants arrived from Europe. Some came to escape poverty at home, some to find freedom from oppressive laws. America's reputation as a land of opportunity spread far and wide.

## Alaska and Hawaii

In the latter part of the nineteenth century, the United States acquired two more territories that would eventually become states. Alaska was purchased from Russia in 1867. The U.S. government annexed Hawaii in 1898.

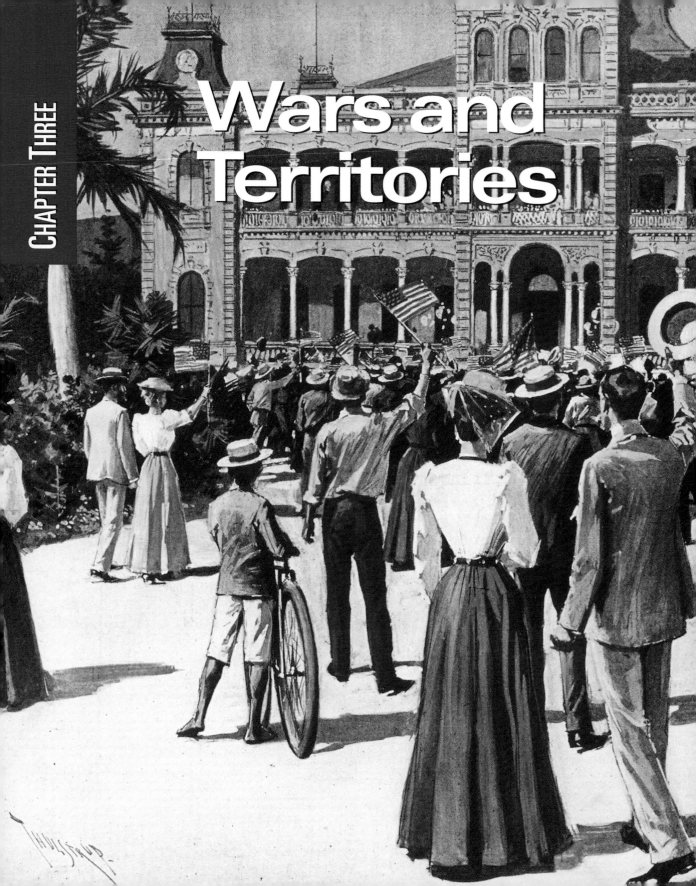

# CHAPTER THREE

# Wars and Territories

Native huts on the Hawaiian island of Kauai in the 1800s

The United States celebrated its 100th birthday in good shape. Americans were feeling proud. The nation stretched across the continent, and all the territories were growing rapidly toward achieving statehood.

The U.S. Bureau of the Census stated in 1880 that America had no more frontier land. There were pockets of settlement all the way across the nation. Some political leaders wanted to look beyond the Pacific Coast. If the frontier had reached the ocean, where could it go from there? The progress and success of the United States in the nineteenth century had been achieved through expansion—a growing population, a healthy flow of immigrants, and the development of new markets.

Opposite: Hawaiians receiving news of their U.S. annexation in 1898

European nations—especially Great Britain, Germany, and Spain—had been concentrating on empire building for several centuries. Americans were divided in their opinions about imperialism. Because the United States was born of a revolution against colonialism, many people felt that acquiring and ruling a foreign territory would be a violation of the national ideal of self-government. Others were convinced that it was necessary to acquire more territory in order to expand international trade and establish military bases.

## The Hawaiian Islands

For decades, Americans had been interested in the Sandwich Islands (now the state of Hawaii). Clipper ships on long Pacific voyages used them as a stopover. Whalers made profitable use of their waters. Missionaries from New England landed on the islands in 1820, and other American settlers—mainly seamen, whalers, and planters—soon followed.

In 1859, an American captain discovered an uninhabited group of tiny islands within an atoll about 1,300 miles (2,092 kilometers) northwest of Honolulu. (An atoll is a circular coral reef surrounding a lagoon.) American companies hoped to use the islands as a stopover on transpacific voyages. The United States annexed Midway Atoll, as the reef was later named in 1867, and sent a naval captain to take possession of it in 1869. Not much happened on Midway for many years.

Sugarcane was a major crop in the Hawaiian Islands. In 1875, the United States signed an agreement not to tax Hawaiian sugar. This treaty, in effect, made the islands an American protectorate, partially controlled by the United States. In 1887, the island rulers gave the United States the right to establish a naval base at Pearl Harbor, on the island of Oahu.

Four years later, the Hawaiian king died. He was succeeded by his sister, Queen Liliuokalani, who did not want the islands to be controlled by foreign interests. The American residents were alarmed. They led a revolution against the queen, and for six years Hawaii was an independent republic.

In 1898, during the Spanish-American War, Congress voted to annex Hawaii as a territory. The United States had now expanded beyond the continental limits.

Queen Liliuokalani worried that Hawaii would be controlled by foreign interests.

## War with Spain

Those in the United States who wanted to expand also had their eyes on certain islands held by Spain in the Pacific Ocean and the Caribbean Sea. Preaching the popular principle of Manifest Destiny, they boasted that Americans were God's chosen people who had a duty go forth and rescue the downtrodden people from their

### Labels

Americans have always been quick to pin labels on people with whom they disagree. Those who want to preserve peace have been called isolationists, or "doves." Sometimes, if war fever grows, they are thought to be either cowardly or unpatriotic.

During the late nineteenth century, Americans who wanted to acquire more territory were known as expansionists. A slang word, "jingo," came from a popular tune. Jingoism stood for aggressive patriotism. More recently, pro-war advocates have been known as "hawks." ■

harsh Spanish rulers. Among the leaders who spoke out in favor of colonies were Senator Henry Cabot Lodge of Massachusetts, diplomat John Hay, and Theodore Roosevelt, who later became president of the United States.

## "Remember the *Maine*"

Cuba, the largest island in the Caribbean Sea, lies about 90 miles (145 km) south of Florida. Cuba was one of Spain's most important colonies. In 1890, a severe depression caused widespread poverty on the island. A rebellion against Spain broke out in 1895. Cuban immigrants in the United States conducted a campaign of anti-Spanish propaganda and sent support to the guerrilla fighters in Cuba.

**The *Maine* arriving in Havana, Cuba**

The Spanish governor of Cuba used cruel measures to put down the revolt. Americans, inflamed by the news of atrocities in Cuba, grew angry and uneasy. Before long, an incident in the harbor of Havana, Cuba, propelled the United States into war with Spain.

In January 1898, the U.S. battleship *Maine* was sent to Havana. The mission was supposed to ensure that American lives and property in Cuba were protected. However, a large

## Theodore Roosevelt

Theodore Roosevelt was born in 1858 into an aristocratic New York family. His parents were shocked when he decided to go into politics. A political career, they felt, was not a respectable pursuit for a person of their class.

Roosevelt served in the state legislature and became active in the Republican Party. He supported William McKinley's campaign for the presidency of the United States. When McKinley was elected and took office in 1897, McKinley named Roosevelt assistant secretary of the U.S. Navy.

President McKinley hoped to avoid war with Spain, but Roosevelt was an outspoken hawk and expansionist. He criticized the president for lacking the courage to go to war. After the Spanish-American conflict had ended, Roosevelt called it "a splendid little war."

"Teddy" Roosevelt got a lot of publicity for leading a cavalry regiment called the Rough Riders against Spanish forces in Cuba. He became a hero in the eyes of the American people. McKinley ran for a second term in 1900, with Roosevelt on the ticket as the Republican nominee for vice president.

Only six months after his inauguration, McKinley was assassinated, and Theodore Roosevelt became the twenty-sixth president of the United States. He was only forty-two years old. He was returned to office in 1904 by the largest majority ever up to that time. In 1912, after four years out of office, Roosevelt ran again for the presidency, but this time he lost. ■

explosion on February 15 destroyed the ship in the harbor. Two hundred and sixty officers and men were on board.

Although no one ever found out who or what caused the explosion, the American public quickly jumped to the conclusion that Spaniards were responsible. Theodore Roosevelt and his friends had no trouble whipping up enthusiasm for going to war with Spain. Soon, newspaper headlines, popular songs, and people in everyday conversation were repeating the slogan, "Remember the *Maine.*"

Roosevelt told President William McKinley that going to war was the only decision "compatible with our national honor." Congress soon passed a declaration of intention to liberate the island of Cuba by force. Added to the declaration was the Teller Amendment, proposed by a senator from Colorado. It stated that the United States had no intention of ruling over Cuba and pledged that control of the island would be left to the Cubans. In spite of this amendment, however, Cuba was governed by an American military administration until 1902.

A few days after the *Maine* exploded, Congress officially declared war against Spain. The first military action took place not in the Caribbean but in the Philippine Islands in the Pacific Ocean. Commodore George Dewey sailed into Manila Bay and destroyed the Spanish fleet there.

By July, Spanish forces in Cuba surrendered and, by August, they had also given up the Philippines. U.S. forces also invaded Puerto Rico, where they met little resistance.

In an armistice signed on August 12, 1898, Spain gave up its claims to Cuba, Puerto Rico, and a Pacific island later known as Guam. Negotiations over the Philippines continued until a treaty was signed in Paris on December 10, 1898. In February of the next year, Congress ratified the treaty with a margin of only one vote.

Although the warfare had lasted less than four months, the conflict forever changed the lives of many people on several far-flung islands. The Treaty of Paris guaranteed independence for Cuba. The Philippines, Puerto Rico, and Guam were ceded to the United States.

## American Samoa

Another group of small Pacific islands became territories of the United States in 1899. Seven islands are clustered in the South Pacific Ocean about 4,800 miles (7,723 km) southwest of San Francisco. Formerly called the Navigators Islands, they were often used as a stopover point for traders sailing between North America and Australia. Germany, the United States, and Great Britain were all interested in keeping the islands open for trade and for

The Battle of Manila Bay during the Spanish-American War

possible military bases. In 1872, the United States acquired the right to establish a naval station at the port of Pago Pago (pronounced *PAHNG-oh PAHNG-oh*) on the island of Tutuila.

The three powerful countries made an agreement in 1899 to control the Samoan islands through a joint protectorate. They also agreed that Samoans would retain the right to govern themselves. Ten years later, Britain pulled out of the agreement and the Samoan islands were divided between Germany and the United States. Germany took over the two largest Samoan islands; the United States got the smaller islands to the east.

## The New Century

As the 1900s began, America's expansionists looked back on a victorious decade. The nation's borders no longer ended at the shores of North America. The United States now had control over the Philippines, Guam, part of Samoa, and the Hawaiian Islands in the Pacific, as well as Puerto Rico in the Caribbean Sea.

The United States had become a colonial power. This was a very confusing situation. The U.S. Constitution had set no rules for administering overseas colonies. Orderly procedures were in place for setting up incorporated territories and eventually admitting them as states, equal to other states already in the Union. (Hawaii and Alaska fit into that pattern—although the twentieth century would be half over before they were admitted as states.) So, with no precedents to follow, governmental matters in the newly acquired colonies were settled in a hit-or-miss fashion by acts of Congress and Supreme Court decisions. From these acts a theory evolved that island possessions are dependencies of, but not part of, the United States. Their inhabitants would not be U.S. citizens unless Congress specifically granted them that status.

## The Philippines

The Philippine people were not necessarily happy to have exchanged Spanish rule for that of the United States. Many of them wanted total independence, and they were willing to fight for it. Warfare continued in the islands between Filipino and American soldiers for many more months. These bloody battles were more devastating and costly than the war with Spain had been.

On July 4, 1901, William Howard Taft, who would later become president of the United States, was sworn in as the first American civil governor of the islands. An elected assembly was to be the legislative branch of the Philippine government.

Political leaders in the United States promised eventual independence for the Philippines. A law was passed in 1934 creating the Commonwealth of the Philippines and providing for a ten-year transition to independence. However, the outbreak of World War II postponed that process. Japan attacked the islands on December 8, 1941, and occupied them until the end of the war in 1945. On July 4, 1946, Congress declared the independence of the Republic of the Philippines.

**William Howard Taft was the first American governor of the Philippines.**

## Puerto Rico

Puerto Rico's relationship with the United States is unique. A government set up by Congress in 1900 provided for a two-house legislature. Puerto Ricans would elect members of the lower house; the U.S. government would appoint members of the upper house

The city of Ponce, Puerto Rico, in the 1890s

and a governor. A nonvoting delegate would represent Puerto Rico in the U.S. House of Representatives.

Puerto Rican citizens were given U.S. citizenship in 1917. In 1952, Congress established the Commonwealth of Puerto Rico. Today, some Puerto Ricans want their land to become a U.S. state; others argue for independence. Neither side has acquired enough support to accomplish its goal.

## Acquisitions in the Twentieth Century

The flags of Spain, Britain, France, the Netherlands, Denmark, and Sweden have flown over various islands in the Caribbean Sea. Except for Puerto Rico, the United States did not claim any land in this region until 1917, when America bought three islands—St.

Thomas, St. John, and St. Croix—from Denmark. The United States purchased these islands at a very high price because of the islands' strategic military importance.

St. John was one of the three Virgin Islands acquired from Denmark in 1917.

More Pacific islands were acquired after World War II ended in 1945. Some of them were battle sites during that war. One strategic group of islands was the Marianas, located about 3,700 miles (5,954 km) west of the Hawaiian Islands. Guam, the largest and southernmost island in the archipelago, or chain of islands, had been a territory of the United States since the end of the Spanish-American War. In 1947, the United Nations Security Council created the Trust Territory of the Pacific Islands and placed the remaining Mariana Islands in the care of the United States. The islands became self-governing in 1978. The United States terminated its trusteeship

## World War II in the Pacific

Many of the thousands of islands in the western Pacific Ocean are quite small and have few residents. However, they became quite important during World War II. Soon after Japan attacked Pearl Harbor, Japanese troops seized several islands that had been administered by the United States since the end of the Spanish-American War. First, Guam and Wake Island surrendered to Japan; then Japan took over Manila in the Philippines.

For the next 3 1/2 years, battles between the Allied troops and Japan were fought on dozens of Pacific Islands. The Pacific Theater, as the battle area was called, included islands between Japan on the north and Australia on the south, and from Midway Atoll on the east to Singapore and Indonesia on the west.

Japan occupied many of these islands for much of the war, until U.S. forces won them back. In 1947, the United Nations created the Trust Territory of the Pacific Islands and gave the trusteeship to the United States. A governor and a territorial congress administered the territory until the early 1990s.

The Trust Territory covered an area as large as the United States, although the land area was only about 717 square miles (1,857 sq km). It included the Marshall, Caroline, and Mariana Islands, with a total population of about 50,000. ■

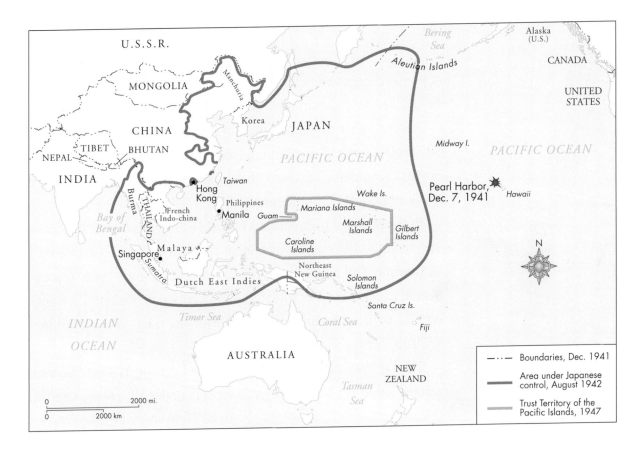

The Pacific Theater during World War II

in 1990, and the islands became the Commonwealth of the Northern Mariana Islands, in political union with the United States. Most of its residents were granted U.S. citizenship.

The Marshall Islands, a German possession until World War I (1914–1918), were then administered by Japan under a League of Nations mandate. After World War II, they became part of the Trust Territory under the administration of the United States. The Republic of the Marshall Islands was recognized as an independent nation in 1991, with a compact of free association with the United States.

For centuries, the Caroline Islands had been ruled in turn by Spain, Germany, Japan, and then the United States, under the Trust Territory of the Pacific Islands. In 1991, the region became

Opposite: The Mariana Islands are in political union with the United States.

recognized internationally as the Federated States of Micronesia, also in free association with the United States.

Several other tiny atolls that lie west and southwest of Hawaii are administered by the United States. These reefs are composed mostly of volcanic or coral rock, have little or no soil, and are nearly or entirely uninhabited.

Wake Island, which consists of three atolls, has been a U.S. possession since 1898 and is administered by the U.S. Department of the Interior. The U.S. Navy ran Midway Island until 1966. A presidential executive order transferred control to the Fish and Wildlife Service of the Department of Interior, as part of the National Wildlife Refuge system.

The Defense Nuclear Agency and the Fish and Wildlife Service manage Johnston Atoll. Kingman Reef is under U.S. Navy control.

The Department of the Interior administers all the islands of Howland, Jarvis, and Baker, as well as Palmyra Atoll.

An uninhabited island called Navassa lies on the other side of the world, 100 miles (160 km) south of Cuba in the Caribbean Sea. It covers 2 square miles (5.2 sq km) and is controlled by the Fish and Wildlife Service. The U.S. Coast Guard maintained a lighthouse there until 1996.

**A seal lion on Jarvis Island**

## U.S. Territories and Associated Regions as of 2000
### (Uninhabited islands are not included.)

### Commonwealth of the Northern Mariana Islands
Self-governing commonwealth in political union with the United States.
  Population estimate: 69,398

### Commonwealth of Puerto Rico
Self-governing commonwealth with a nonvoting representative in U.S. Congress. Puerto Rican citizens also have U.S. citizenship.
  Population estimate: 3,887,652

### Midway Island
Unincorporated and unorganized territory of the United States, administered by the U.S. Department of the Interior.
  Population estimate: About 450 government workers

### Republic of the Marshall Islands
Constitutional government in free association with the United States.
  Population estimate: 65,507

### Territory of American Samoa
Unincorporated and unorganized territory of the United States, administered by the U.S. Department of the Interior.
  Population estimate: 63,786

### Territory of Guam
Organized, unincorporated territory of the United States, administered by the U.S. Department of the Interior.
  Population estimate: 151,716

### Virgin Islands of the United States
Organized, unincorporated territory of the United States, administered by the U.S. Department of the Interior.
  Population estimate: 119,827

### Wake Island
Unincorporated and unorganized territory of the United States, administered by the U.S. Department of the Interior.
  Population estimate: About 200 civilian contract workers

# CHAPTER FOUR

# Pacific Islands: The Natural Setting

The Pacific Ocean is the largest body of water on Earth—larger than all the land on all the continents combined. North and South America are east of the Pacific while Asia and Australia lie to the west. More than 25,000 islands are scattered over this great expanse. The great majority of these islands are in the western part of the ocean, closer to Asia and Australia than to the Americas.

This huge, uncharted ocean fascinated early European explorers. Marco Polo of Italy traveled to China during the late thirteenth century and saw the ocean. More than 200 years later, a Portuguese explorer, Ferdinand Magellan, sailed across the vast sea. He found calm seas and fair weather with warm winds. He decided to name the waters the Pacific Ocean. The word *pacific* means "calm and peaceful," and that's how Magellan saw the ocean when he chose the name. Since then, however, thousands of sailors have found that this huge ocean is often anything but peaceful. Huge tropical storms called typhoons have destroyed countless ships and human lives. Geographers divide the ocean into the North and South Pacific; the equator is the dividing line.

In the 1700s, a British naval officer named Captain James Cook sailed across the Pacific three times. He was the first European to discover some of the islands, including those now in the state of Hawaii, and he also produced the first reliable map of the Pacific Ocean.

Marco Polo

**Opposite: The rugged coast of Wake Island**

## The Pacific Islands

The islands of the western Pacific are generally divided into three groups—Micronesia, meaning "small islands," Polynesia, meaning "many islands," and Melanesia, meaning "dark islands." Together, these three groups are known as the Pacific Islands. Micronesia lies almost entirely north of the equator. Melanesia and Polynesia lie on both sides of the equator. Samoa and the Hawaiian Islands, including Midway, are in Polynesia. The other inhabited islands that have, or had, a relationship with the United States are in Micronesia.

## Micronesia

Micronesia includes about 2,500 pieces of land scattered about 500 miles (805 km) east of the Philippines and west of the International Date Line, an imaginary line running from the North Pole to the South Pole that separates the calendar date on either side. Together, these islands make up less than 4 percent of the total land area of the Pacific Islands. They include several groups—the Marianas, the Marshalls, the Carolines, and the Gilberts.

Wake Island, a small and almost uninhabited island north of the Marshalls, is another U.S. possession in Micronesia. Its strategic location in the North Pacific has made it useful for the emergency landing of aircraft. There are no permanent residents, but the U.S. Army conducts occasional activities there.

Some tiny Pacific Islands are merely piles of sand or coral reefs with little vegetation. Others, especially the larger ones, are hilly or even mountainous, covered with thick forests and other plant life. Some shorelines have sandy beaches and palm trees;

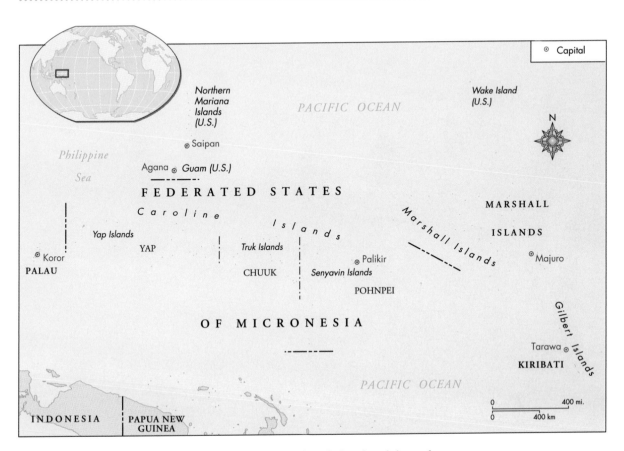

Micronesia

others are mostly mangrove swamps. Much of the land is volcanic lava and ash. In areas where rainfall is plentiful, water has seeped through the limestone rock and created caves.

The Northern Marianas are actually the peaks of a huge mountain range that rises up from the bottom of the Mariana Trench—the deepest known spot in the oceans of the world. The tops of the mountains rise up more than 6 miles (10 km) from the bottom of the trench. According to some geologists, these areas may once have been part of a huge continent that extended from Asia to the islands of the South Pacific.

Guam has a great variety of plants in its interior areas.

Guam, the largest island in the Marianas group, is about 30 miles (48 km) long and 4 to 8 miles (6 to 13 km) wide. Its total area is 217 square miles (562 sq km). In the north, a steep coastline rises to a forested plateau. The bedrock is coral limestone. There are some rivers and volcanic hills in the south. Palm trees, pandanus (screw pine), and other trees grow along the coast. The hills are covered with sword grass.

For most of the year, the climate is tropical—hot and humid. Trade winds cool the temperature slightly from December to April.

**Guam's Geographical Features**

| | |
|---|---|
| **Total area** | 217 sq. mi. (562 sq km) |
| **Land** | 210 sq. mi. (544 sq km) |
| **Highest point** | Mount Lamlam, Agat District, 1,332 feet (406 m) |
| **Lowest point** | Sea level at the Pacific Ocean |
| **Largest city** | Agana |
| **Population** | 151,716 (estimate) |
| **Average temperatures** | 70°F to 90°F (21°C to 32°C) |
| **Average annual rainfall** | 90 inches (229 cm) |

The wet season—July to November—sometimes brings destructive typhoons.

Bats and lizards are just about the only native wildlife in the Marianas. The wild pigs and deer that are seen occasionally were brought in by early voyagers.

## Polynesia

Polynesia is the largest section of the Pacific Islands. If you draw a large triangle with the three points at Midway Atoll in the north, Easter Island in the southeast, and New Zealand in the southwest, you will have a rough idea of where Polynesia is. Midway and American Samoa are not the only U.S. territories in Polynesia. Other U.S. possessions include Johnston and Palmyra Atolls, Kingman Reef, and Howland, Baker, and Jarvis Islands.

The Samoan islands are about 4,800 miles (7,723 km) southwest of San Francisco, California. The nine western islands make up the independent island nation of Samoa. The seven eastern islands make up the Territory of American Samoa.

## Midway Atoll

Midway was the first overseas possession of the United States. An attempt to improve the channel into the islands failed because the surrounding reef was made of solid limestone. In 1903, U.S. companies built a relay station there for transpacific cable communication. During the 1930s, the U.S. Marines built facilities for naval and air defense. Before jet planes were used for air travel, Midway was a stopping point for aircraft en route to the Philippines.

During World War II, Midway was the site of an important naval battle. The U.S. victory over Japan at Midway was a turning point in the war. Today, a naval ghost town stands at the battle site.

In 1996, Midway was declared a National Wildlife Refuge. Control was transferred from the U.S. Navy to the Fish and Wildlife Service of the Department of Interior. Tourists come to watch the million or so gooney birds who live there (above). These seabirds, properly called black-footed albatrosses, "own" the islands. They don't make way for human intruders on the ground and, with a wingspread of more than 6 feet (2 m) and a squawk that sounds like applause, they rule the sky, too. Some fifteen other species of seabirds share the islands, but they are greatly outnumbered by the gooneys.

Large monk seals—an endangered species—and spinner dolphins are among the protected wildlife on Midway. The Fish and Wildlife Service is working to restore the little islands to their natural state. They have succeeded in eliminating the rats that were accidentally brought in by service personnel during the war. The Fish and Wildlife Service hopes to have similar success in getting rid of nonnative plants. ▪

## American Samoa

The largest island in American Samoa is Tutuila. Its 53 square miles (137 sq km) make up almost 70 percent of the total land area on all seven islands. Pago Pago, on the southeastern coast of Tutuila, is the territorial capital and chief port. Spectacular mountains rise up all around the harbor. Aunuu Island, a small volcanic crater, lies just offshore. Three other especially beautiful islands are the Manua group—Upolu, Olosego, and Ofu—about 65 miles (105 km) east of Tutuila.

**Pago Pago is the main harbor on the island of Tutuila.**

## American Samoa's Geographical Features

| | |
|---|---|
| **Total area** | 90 sq. mi. (233 sq km) |
| **Land** | 77 sq. mi. (199 sq km) |
| **Highest point** | Lata Mountain, Upolu Island, 3,160 feet (964 m) |
| **Lowest point** | Sea level at the Pacific Ocean |
| **Largest city** | Pago Pago |
| **Population** | 63,786 (estimate) |
| **Average temperatures** | 70°F to 90°F (21°C to 32°C) |
| **Average annual rainfall** | 200 inches (508 cm) |

The flying fox is also called a fruit bat.

The peaks and ridges of American Samoa are extensively weathered and eroded. Some of the craters formed by volcanoes have already crumbled into the sea. One still-active volcano is submerged south of the Manua Islands.

Two privately owned coral atolls—Rose and Swains Islands—are nesting grounds for many seabirds. Access to these islands is restricted and controlled by the U.S. Fish and Wildlife Service.

The Samoan islands have a variety of plants but little animal life. There are some snakes and lizards and a most unusual fruit bat called the flying fox. The bat's wings stretch to as much as 3 feet (1 meter). Fruit bats are important to the ecosystem—they pollinate and scatter the seeds of many tropical plants. In the past, Samoans exported these creatures to Guam, where they were prized for food. They are now protected in Samoa and American Samoa.

Seabirds, including boobies, frigate birds, and terns, live on cliffs along the shore. From time to time, dolphins, whales, turtles, and sharks can be spotted swimming nearby. A local legend says that a shark and a turtle will appear whenever a group of children sings on one of the beaches of Tutuila.

## National Park of American Samoa

The National Park of American Samoa was established in 1988. In 1993, the U.S. government signed a fifty-year lease for land on Tutuila, Upolu, and Ofu. The park service manages the 9,000 acres (3,645 ha) of land and 480 acres (194 ha) of offshore waters, but the Samoans who live there own them. The people of nine villages within the park practice traditional agriculture.

The park has four distinct types of rain forest, and many lovely waterfalls, coral reefs, and beaches. The park also contains the highest point in American Samoa, Mount Lata, which rises to 3,160 feet (964 m). Hundreds of different plant species and two species of flying foxes live in the park. There is one short hiking trail in the park, but more are being planned. ■

The climate of the Samoan islands is tropical—hot, humid, and often rainy. Earthquakes and typhoons are frequent. The region suffered extensive storm damage in 1987, and again in 1990. Then, in December 1991, "the planet's worst storm in living memory," according to news reports, caused damage estimated at $80 million. The greatest destruction was on the island of Savaii, in the independent state of Samoa.

# CHAPTER FIVE

# Guam and American Samoa: History, Government, Economy

The Portuguese explorer Ferdinand Magellan sighted the island of Guam during his voyage around the world in 1521. Spain took possession of the Mariana Islands, including the island of Guam, in 1565. Spain then governed Guam as a part of the Philippines.

U.S. troops recaptured Guam in 1944.

The United States took over Guam after the Spanish-American War. The U.S. Navy established a naval base there and controlled the island until 1941. Japanese military forces seized the island at the start of World War II and held it until August 1944, when American forces recaptured it. The battle destroyed Agana, the capital, and devastated much of the island. In 1962, a disastrous typhoon did even greater damage. More than 90 percent of the buildings were ruined, nine people were killed, and two towns were completely destroyed. Another devastating typhoon struck in 1992.

In 1950, the administration of Guam was transferred from the U.S. Navy to the Department of the Interior under the Organic Act of Guam. A civilian government was established at that time.

Until 1970, the U.S. president appointed the governor of Guam. Since then, territorial elections have been held to choose a governor, who serves for four years. The governor appoints department heads with the consent of the legislature. Guam's legislature con-

Opposite: Agana, the capital city of Guam

**Guam's Official Song
"Guam Hymn"**

Written by Dr. Ramon Sablan

Stand ye Guamanians, for your
    country,
And sing her praise from shore
    to shore.
For her honor, for her glory,
Exalt our Island forever more.
For her honor, for her glory,
Exalt our Island forever more.
May everlasting peace reign
    o'er us,

May heaven's blessings to
    us come.
Against all perils, do not
    forsake us,
God protect our Isle of Guam.
Against all perils, do not
    forsake us,
God protect our Isle of Guam.

sists of one house, with twenty-one elected members who serve two-year terms. The district court of Guam settles judicial matters, which can be reviewed by the U.S. Court of Appeals and the U.S. Supreme Court.

Legally, Guam is classified as an organized, unincorporated territory of the United States. All Guamanians over eighteen years old are U.S. citizens, eligible to vote in local, but not presidential, elections. One nonvoting delegate represents Guam in the U.S. House of Representatives.

## Guam's Economy

The economy of Guam depends heavily on the U.S. military installations located there. The U.S. Navy, Air Force, Marines, and Coast Guard all have troops stationed on Guam. Andersen Air Force Base on the island's northeastern plateau is a major U.S. defense base. Together, the air force and navy operate a research, reconnaissance, and forecasting facility called the Joint Typhoon Warning Center.

The island has few natural resources. Some residents have small gardens and ranches, where they grow vegetables and fruits and raise poultry, hogs, cattle, and water buffalo. However, most of the islanders' food is imported. The waters around Guam have a good supply of fish, but commercial fishing is not highly developed.

Small factories process food, assemble watches, and manufacture furniture, tobacco products, and alcoholic beverages. International communication includes underwater cable and radio. Local radio and television stations, plus newspapers, keep the people informed.

More than a million tourists visit Guam each year, most of them from Japan. Good accommodations, lovely tropical scenery and climate, and duty-free shopping attract them. They also appreciate interesting prehistoric sites and historic ruins. A dozen major international airlines and several shipping lines provide service. Tourism is of great importance to the island.

**Territorial Flag of Guam**

The territorial flag is a rectangle with a dark-blue field and a narrow red border on all four sides. In the center, a red-bordered, pointed, vertical ellipse frames a tropical scene. A palm tree stands on a beach overlooking the ocean, and an outrigger canoe floats on the water. The word *Guam* appears across the picture in red letters. ■

## What Guam Grows and Manufactures

| Agriculture | Manufacturing |
| --- | --- |
| Bananas | Cement |
| Coconuts | Furniture |
| Sugarcane | Plastics |
| Sweet potatoes | Textiles |
| Taro | |

Guam's natural beauty
attracts visitors from
all over the world.

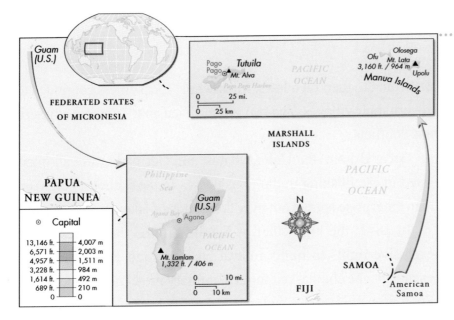

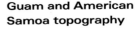

Guam and American Samoa topography

## American Samoa

Pirates and whalers sailing in the Pacific were among the first Europeans to visit Samoa. By the mid-nineteenth century, Pago Pago was one of the prime whaling ports in the entire Pacific.

By the early 1800s, European traders made frequent stops at these islands. The traders were on their way to China, carrying whale products and sandalwood to exchange for silks, tea, and porcelain. Some of them liked the climate and scenery of the South Pacific so much that they settled there. Sadly, they brought some unwelcome guests with them—European diseases to which the natives had no immunity. A number of Europeans settled in the Samoan islands in the next few decades. They established their own communities and lived

European whalers often made stops in the Samoan islands.

**American Samoan Flag**

The territorial flag is blue with a white triangle edged in red. A flying brown-and-white American bald eagle carries two Samoan symbols of authority—a staff and a war club. ■

according to their own laws. Meanwhile, local chiefs continued to govern their villages. The two groups lived apart, without any serious conflicts.

Great Britain, the United States, and Germany were all interested in establishing trading businesses in the Samoas. One German enterprise spread out over thousands of islands in the Pacific.

In 1872, the high chief of Tutuila offered the United States exclusive rights to build a naval base in Pago Pago Harbor. In exchange, the chief asked for U.S. military protection of the island. Soon after this, a U.S. colonel in Samoa broke off ties with the United States and started private negotiations with Germany.

Great Britain, the United States, and Germany each wanted to protect its own interests in the islands. All three nations sent warships to Apia Harbor (in present-day independent Samoa). But a huge typhoon prevented open warfare among the nations.

In 1900, all the chiefs in the eastern Samoan islands agreed to give the U.S. Navy authority to govern and protect the region. The Samoan people were declared U.S. nationals, and the territory was officially named American Samoa in 1905.

American Samoa is an unorganized, unincorporated territory of the United States. Unlike the residents of the territories of Guam and the U.S. Virgin Islands, American Samoans are U.S. nationals, but they are not citizens of the United States. The territory has its own constitution, in effect since 1967. All people over age eighteen can vote in local elections. They also vote for a representative to the U.S. Congress, who can take part in debates in the House, but has no vote except in committee.

As U.S. nationals, American Samoans have freedom of entry

**Waiting for a bus in Pago Pago**

into the United States and may apply for U.S. citizenship. However, Samoans are no longer permitted to move freely between American Samoa and the independent state of Samoa.

Like most U.S. states and territories, the government of American Samoa is divided into three branches: executive, legislative, and judicial. The governor and lieutenant governor are elected for four-year terms. The legislature, called the Fono, has two sections—a senate and a house of representatives. There are eighteen senators, elected from local chiefs for four-year terms. The house has twenty-one members. Twenty are elected for two-year terms, and one is appointed as a nonvoting delegate from the privately owned Swains Island.

The judicial branch of government consists of village courts, district courts, and the High Court. The U.S. secretary of the interior appoints the chief justice and associate justices of the High

## What American Samoa Grows and Manufactures

| Agriculture | Manufacturing |
|---|---|
| Bananas | Tuna canning |
| Coconuts | |
| Taro | |

Court. The district courts are made up of Samoan chiefs, who are appointed to the bench by the governor of Samoa.

## Economy of American Samoa

Samoans traditionally have common ownership of land, and 90 percent of the land in American Samoa is communally (collectively) owned. Local farmers raise vegetables, taro, yams, and copra. Tropical fruits such as bananas, coconuts, breadfruit, pineapples, and papayas are plentiful. There is also some dairy farming.

The federal government employs about one-third of the workforce. Tuna fishing and processing are the major industries. Canned tuna is the territory's most important export. Another one-third of the working people have jobs in the canneries. The remainder of Samoa's people work in retail and service industries.

The United States is the principal trading partner for American Samoa. Products exported from the territory to the states are admitted duty-free. This disturbs many people because federal minimum-wage laws are not recognized in the territory.

Samoa is heavily dependent on the U.S. government for financial aid. In the 1960s, the government tried to boost the economy by building roads, housing, transportation facilities, and schools

**Picking coconuts in American Samoa**

and other public buildings. Some Samoan leaders felt that all this activity resulted in too much dependency on welfare and other government assistance.

# CHAPTER SIX

# Guam and American Samoa: The People and Everyday Life

Latte Park in Agana

**A**ncient peoples in Guam built huge pillars of coral called Latte Stones. They look like mushrooms with very long stems. Some scientists think they were used to support the homes of the upper classes. Although their origin is a mystery, they stand as evidence of a long-forgotten culture that once flourished here.

Archaeologists have found artifacts and other evidence that point to settlement on the island as early as 3000 B.C. These settlers are believed to have come from other islands in what are now the Philippines and the Indonesian archipelago. The evidence shows that they lived in villages and cultivated rice, like other East Asian peoples. Guam's population was probably between 50,000 and 75,000 when European explorers arrived.

Opposite: The War Memorial on Marine Drive in Guam

More than 150,000 people live on the tropical island of Guam today. Migration from Asia and other Pacific islands has created a rich and interesting combination of cultures. Native Guamanians are a mixture of Chamorros—a Micronesian group with their own language and culture—with Spanish, Filipino, Mexican, and other early settlers. More recent immigrants include Chinese, Japanese, Koreans, Europeans, Hawaiians, and people from the Americas. Most of those from the United States are military personnel.

English is the official language of Guam, although many older Guamanians still speak Chamorro. The children of Guam from ages six to sixteen are required to attend public or parochial schools. Vocational schools and special facilities for the education of handicapped youngsters are also provided. The University of Guam is a four-year accredited college with a graduate division.

Guam was a colony of Spain for 300 years, and the Spanish left their mark on local customs, especially on religion. Guam was one of the first Pacific islands settled by Europeans. Spanish missionaries came to the island in 1668, and today about 80 percent of the people are Roman Catholics. Most of the rest are Protestants.

Agana, Guam's largest town and territorial capital, has just more than 1,000 people, including outlying residential areas. Government structures, as well as a cathedral, a library, and a historical museum, are all located in Agana. The island's chief port, Apra Harbor, is on the west coast, about 5 miles (8 km) south of the city. Other principal settlements—Sinajana, Tamuning, and Barrigada—are in the center of the island.

## The Samoa Islands

The people of American Samoa and its neighbor, the independent state of Samoa, share a common culture, heritage, and language. Samoans are Polynesians, and all Polynesian languages, including Samoan and Hawaiian, are related to one another.

Archaeological evidence indicates that people lived in the Samoa Islands as long ago as 1000 B.C. Traditionally, Samoans have believed that their ancestors were the first Polynesians, created by the god Tagaloa. Anthropologists, however, think that Polyne-

The governor's complex in Guam is home to the executive branch of government.

## Star Mounds

More than 100 earth and stone mounds built by prehistoric people are scattered across the Samoa Islands. The mounds are roughly star-shaped, with points radiating out from the center. Archaeologists believe the ancient inhabitants used the mounds for sport and religion.

Pigeon-snaring was the islanders' major sport. Feasting and partying went along with the hunting games—just as people today get together at football games and horse races. The pigeon-snaring sites were probably also used for important religious rituals. ■

**Ancient traditions are still part of life in American Samoa.**

sians migrated to the islands of the South Pacific from such places as Indonesia, Asia's Malay Peninsula, and the Philippines.

## Samoan People Today

About 63,000 people live in American Samoa, and some 95 percent of them reside on the island of Tutuila. The other 5 percent live on the Manua Islands. The hundreds of foreign residents include Koreans, Chinese, North Americans, Australians, and Europeans. Most of the foreigners hold government jobs or work in education and health care. Foreigners are not permitted to buy land in American Samoa.

Samoans live in villages, as they have for centuries. Each village consists of a group of extended family units. Each family unit is headed by a chief, and the chiefs form the village council. Traditionally, all wealth and land in the village are communally owned. Western ideas of individual property ownership are creeping into the Samoan society, but have not yet become widespread.

Children are required to attend school from ages six to eighteen. There are about thirty free public schools and six private schools. Television is often used as an educational aid in the classroom. Villages provide preschool programs. Nearly all Samoans speak English as a second language.

Some of the sailors who visited Samoa during the nineteenth century told the people about Christianity. The Samoans accepted much of what they heard because the Christian version of the creation of the world was much like the one they already believed. Protestant missionaries visited the islands in the 1820s and 1830s; French Catholic priests arrived in 1845. Today, the

**A village school in American Samoa**

## Samoan Language

Samoan is a Polynesian language. It is not spoken anywhere else in Polynesia, but it has similarities to Maori, Tongan, Hawaiian, and Tahitian. Some words are much like Malay, which leads scholars to think that early Malaysians migrated to Samoa.

The Samoan alphabet has only five vowels and nine consonants. Here are a few Samoan words:

|  |  |
|---|---|
| *malo* | hello |
| *tofa* | good-bye |
| *fa'amolemole* | please |
| *fa'afetai* | thank you |
| *masalo* | maybe |
| *ua ou sese* | I'm sorry |
| *tama* | boy |
| *teine* | girl |
| *palagi* | foreigner |

major religious denominations in the Samoas are Congregational, Roman Catholic, Methodist, and Church of Jesus Christ of Latter-day Saints.

## Pago Pago

Pago Pago is not a city in the usual sense. It is made up of a large harbor surrounded by several small villages—one of which is named Pago Pago.

The harbor was created when the wall of an ancient volcanic crater collapsed and fell into the ocean. Almost surrounded by land, the harbor is wonderfully well protected from the open ocean. Steep mountains rise straight up from the water, creating a breath-taking tropical scene. Some of the best views are from the top of Mount Alva, north of the harbor. The mountain ridge is part of the National Park of American Samoa.

The village of Fagatogo, on the western side of the harbor, is the capital of the territory. The courthouse and the buildings for the Fono (the legislature) are here. The Jean P. Haydon Museum has an interesting display of early Samoan artifacts and other items related to island life.

**The Fono legislature building in Pago Pago**

## Flowerpot Rocks

Two rock formations along the highway around Pago Pago Harbor are the subject of a local legend. It seems that two young lovers who lived on the Manua islands were forbidden to marry. The woman built a raft and left home, heading for Tutuila. Her lover took off to follow her. A tidal wave destroyed both boats and threw the young lovers onto the rocky land, where they were turned to stone.

It is interesting to find that similar stories are told in societies throughout the world. In countless locations, old stories tell of star-crossed lovers who were transformed into natural landmarks.

## Clothing and Food

While younger Samoans often wear Western-style clothing, traditional clothes are popular too. For men, a piece of brightly patterned cloth is wrapped around the body to form a floor-length skirt. This skirt is called a *lavalava,* and a plain white Western shirt is sometimes worn with it. The equivalent for women is a *puletasi,* also a skirt, topped with a tunic.

Many Samoan men have elaborate tattoos covering them from waist to knees. The patterns are so intricate that the men appear to be wearing knee-length shorts. It takes up to a month to complete the entire process of this kind of tattooing. The practice is not as universal as it once was, but tattoos were traditionally considered a mark of manhood in Samoa.

Food, as well as clothing, has been heavily influenced by international tastes and habits. Burgers and hot dogs, pizza, and Chinese and Korean dishes are common in American Samoa. But traditional Polynesian foods, such as fresh fish, suckling pig, taro, and tropical fruits, are also popular. Coconut cream is used in many Samoan dishes.

Opposite: Traditional clothing in American Samoa is often brightly colored.

## Native Arts

Traditional Samoan houses were built on platforms made of rocks or pebbles and were covered with woven mats. Wooden poles supported the roofs, which were made of thatched coconut fronds. These houses had no walls, but blinds could be pulled down to keep out rain or heavy winds. Today, however, most homes in American Samoa are Western-style structures, with walls and windows and doors.

People in American Samoa live in both traditional and modern homes.

Samoans love to sing, and a great many of them have a talent for music. Samoan folk songs tell stories of love, patriotism, and

## Western Writers and Samoa

son (left) had poor health. He died at the age of forty-four, but left behind a treasury of books such as *Treasure Island* and *Kidnapped* that are enjoyed by both children and adults.

Stevenson spent the last four years of his life in Samoa. The Samoan people loved him, and he was active in the community and on behalf of the rights of the Samoan people. He was honored with funeral rites normally given to chiefs and was buried on top of a mountain on the island of Upolu, Samoa.

The English poet Rupert Brooke (1887–1915) described Samoans as "the loveliest people in the world." In 1928, the American sociologist Margaret Mead (1901–1978) (right) published a book called *Coming of Age in Samoa* about her field

Many European and American writers have been intrigued with the Pacific Islands and their people, especially Samoa. One of the earliest was the Scottish author and poet Robert Louis Stevenson (1850–1894). Steven-

study in the islands. Somerset Maugham (1874–1965), a prolific English writer of plays, novels, and short stories, also wrote about Samoa.

*Tales of the South Pacific,* by James Michener (1907–1997), was a popular book that later became a Broadway musical and a movie. It was one of the first of many best-sellers written by Michener. ▪

important events. Many people enjoy singing in choirs, and brass bands are popular.

Decorative hangings made from the inner bark of the mulberry tree are prized pieces of Samoan artwork. This bark cloth, called *siapo,* is imprinted with intricate designs made with vegetable dyes.

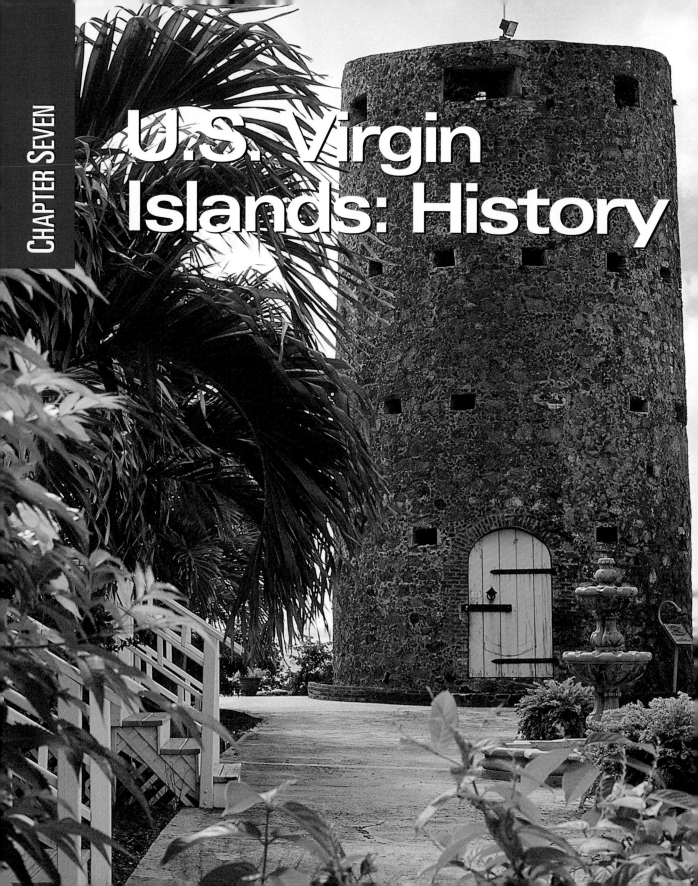

# CHAPTER SEVEN

# U.S. Virgin Islands: History

Christopher Columbus
and his crew on one of
their many voyages

O nly a few people lived on the Caribbean islands before Christopher Columbus arrived in the Americas. He called the people "Indians" because he thought he had reached islands off the coast of Asia, then known as the Indies.

Early South American people migrated in dugout canoes to the islands more than 2,000 years ago. At least three different tribes lived in what are now the Virgin Islands. The Igneri lived there from about A.D. 50 to 650. The Taino (sometimes called Arawak) were here for the next 700 or 800 years. The Carib arrived only a few decades before the Europeans. Early inhabitants made stone tools

Opposite: Blackbeard's
Castle on St. Thomas

Sir Francis Drake stopped in St. Thomas and St. John on his way to Puerto Rico.

and crude pottery. They were good fishers, raised a few crops, and knew how to weave.

Columbus spotted the three islands now known as St. Croix, St. Thomas, and St. John during his second voyage to the Americas, in 1493. Some of his men took a longboat toward the shore of St. Croix. They had a skirmish with some Caribs in a dugout canoe. This is the first documented unfriendly encounter between Europeans and natives.

Columbus named the three islands, along with several dozen smaller islands and cays (low island or reef), the Virgin Islands. The eastern islands have been claimed by Britain since 1672; the western islands were purchased by the United States in 1917.

Columbus was an Italian explorer in the service of the Spanish king and queen. He and his men came ashore on St. Croix, but only briefly. The next known contact with Europeans was almost 100 years later, when Sir Francis Drake, an English sea captain and privateer, stopped at St. Thomas and St. John on his way to Puerto Rico.

In the early 1600s, groups of British, Dutch, and French colonists came to settle St. Croix. Over the next few decades, control of this island passed back and forth between France and Spain. However, the Spaniards were not too interested in these islands because there was no gold to be found.

## Who Were the Virgins?

Columbus chose the name "Virgin Islands" in honor of Saint Ursula, an early Christian martyr. Her story may be largely a legend, and some of the facts have undoubtedly been exaggerated over the centuries.

According to the story, Ursula was the daughter of a Christian king of Britain, born in the third or fourth century. Pagan Huns were threatening to overrun the kingdom, and their leader demanded that Princess Ursula be given to him as a wife. Ursula did not want to marry. She intended to be a nun. She agreed to the marriage, however, in order to save her father's kingdom. But she insisted on certain conditions.

She demanded the right to recruit a group of virgins to live with her for three years before her marriage. Then, according to the legend, she trained her followers as warrior women. But the Hun leader heard about it, and had his own army waiting for the women when they came to his stronghold in Cologne (in what is now Germany). Ursula and all the virgins were killed in that battle.

Perhaps it was the beauty of this group of Caribbean islands that inspired Columbus to name them after the legendary virgins. ∎

## Plantations and Trade

Early colonists built up large plantations on the islands, growing tobacco, cotton, ginger, sugarcane, and indigo. Sugarcane proved to be the most profitable. When the planters needed more people to work in these fields, they began to import African slaves. The first slaves were brought to St. Thomas in 1673.

At about the same time, the Danish West India and Guinea Company claimed St. Thomas and St. John. Soon they changed the name of the main town on St. Thomas to Charlotte Amalie, in honor of the Danish queen. The land on St. Thomas was not good for planting, but its fine harbor made Charlotte Amalie an ideal port for international trade.

The Danes found a way to make their colony profitable through the so-called Triangle Trade. They imported slaves from Africa to

**The harbor at Charlotte Amalie**

work on sugarcane plantations, manufactured molasses from the sugar, processed rum from the molasses, and sold the rum to get money to buy more slaves. Charlotte Amalie was an important slave-trading center for the Caribbean islands.

## Pirates and Privateers

For most of the sixteenth century, the Caribbean islands were used primarily as stopping-off places for traders in gold and silver from Mexico and South America. The Spanish tried to keep all the trade to themselves, but pirates and privateers from other European countries prevented this.

Pirates were sailors who were not interested in trade; they were out to plunder ships carrying valuable cargo. Sometimes identified as the Brotherhood of the Great, they owed allegiance to no one. Privateers, on the other hand, traveled under national flags and were authorized by their respective kings to attack and rob ships from other countries.

Spanish galleons carrying gold did not pass through the Virgin Islands, but St. Thomas was known as a haven for pirates and assorted thieves. One of them was Edward Teach (left), called Blackbeard because of his waist-long facial hair. He is said to have had at least fourteen wives. At one time, Teach supposedly used a tower at the top of a hill in Charlotte Amalie as a hideout. The tower, now a National Historic Landmark, is called Blackbeard's Castle. It is part of a complex with a small hotel and fine restaurant. East of downtown is the hangout of a fictional bearded pirate, Bluebeard's Castle. ■

Denmark then purchased St. Croix. In 1754 the three islands became a royal colony, called the Danish West Indies.

## Slavery

Slaves lived under brutal conditions. They worked hard and long and were treated cruelly. They had no legal rights, and their owners or overseers could punish them for little or no reason. Many died at a young age from starvation, disease, suicide, or violent treatment. The planters simply bought more slaves to take the place of those who died.

This situation persisted throughout the Caribbean islands for more than 100 years. Slaves outnumbered the European settlers on most of the islands, but they had little opportunity to organize any kind of successful rebellion.

On St. John, the forces of nature made conditions even worse. A series of droughts created shortages of food and water. These droughts were followed by severe hurricanes, then by a plague of insects that destroyed even more crops.

Finally, some of the slaves decided they had suffered enough. In 1733, a group of slaves on St. John Island struck back at their oppressors. They managed to seize a fort at Coral Bay, the main settlement on St. John. They fired the cannon at the fort as a signal to other slaves to rebel and attack their masters. For several months, the slaves roamed the island at will, terrifying and immobilizing the planters and their families.

Before the end of the year, however, Danish, Dutch, English, and French soldiers from neighboring islands arrived to stop the rebellion. Within a few months, nearly all the slaves who had taken part in the uprising were killed, either in battle or by execution.

Many of the planters were absentee owners who spent most of their time in Europe. In both Europe and North America, public opinion about slavery was slowly changing. Because of the controversy, the slave trade was beginning to fall apart.

In 1792, the Danish West Indies became the first colony in the Americas to make slave trading illegal. Owners were allowed to keep the slaves they already had, but slave trading ended through-

A group of women catching fish off the coast of St. Thomas

out the Western Hemisphere during the next century. The British banned the ownership of slaves entirely in 1833. They were followed by the Danes and French in 1848, and the Dutch in 1863. Emancipation came to the United States in 1863, two years before the end of the American Civil War. The Spanish outlawed slavery in their South American plantations in Brazil and Cuba in 1888.

The slaves were now free, but they were left in desperate poverty. The sugar-based economy declined. Steamships began to replace sailing vessels, and St. Thomas became less important as a port. During labor riots on St. Croix in 1878, much of the island was burned.

## Emancipation Day

In 1847, the king of Denmark decided to end slavery in the West Indies gradually. However, the slaves in St. Croix wanted action right away. Several thousand of them, under the leadership of a man by the name of Moses "Buddhoe" Gottlieb, gathered together for a march into Frederiksted.

The planters were frightened. The royal governor, Peter von Scholten, decided to act. A kind-hearted man, he sympathized with the slaves. On July 3, 1848, Von Scholten climbed onto the ramparts of Fort Frederik and announced: "All unfree [people] in the Danish West Indies are from today emancipated." Buddhoe and his followers quickly stopped fighting and began to celebrate.

Von Scholten, however, was called back to Copenhagen to face trial for acting without official authority. The government decided to go along with the emancipation, but Von Scholten was never allowed to return to the islands.

A sculpture of Buddhoe is on display in a park named for him next to Fort Frederik. And July 3 is celebrated as Emancipation Day in the U.S. Virgin Islands. ■

U.S. secretary of state William H. Seward negotiated to purchase the Danish West Indies.

## Sale to the United States

During the American Civil War in the United States (1861–1865), U.S. leaders began to be interested in the Caribbean. They felt a naval base in the islands might be necessary for protection of the Atlantic Coast. President Lincoln's secretary of state, William H. Steward, opened negotiations to buy the Danish West Indies. (Seward also negotiated the purchase of Alaska a few years later.) A treaty was signed in 1867 with the approval of the voters of the colony and the Danish parliament. However, a vote in the U.S. Senate failed to ratify the treaty. Congress was deeply divided and distracted by other issues, including an impeachment proceeding.

Then came the Spanish-American War, and further negotiations were delayed until 1900. The Treaty of 1902 was passed by the U.S. Senate this time, but the Danish failed—by one vote—to ratify it. Further negotiations dragged on. The Danes raised the price to five times the original offer, and the United States accepted it. The Danish West Indies became the U.S. Virgin Islands in 1917. The final cost was $290 an acre (0.4 ha)—the highest price ever paid for land by the U.S. government.

## The U.S. Virgin Islands

Economic conditions on the U.S. Virgin Islands were deplorable when the U.S. Navy took over the administration. For several years, little or nothing was done to improve the situation. Unemployment and low wages resulted in widespread poverty. A new series of droughts, a hurricane in 1928, the crash of the stock market in 1929, and a collapse of the sugar industry brought even more hardship and despair.

The residents of the islands had assumed they would be given U.S. citizenship with the takeover, but that did not happen for several years. In 1931, a civilian government replaced control by the navy. The following year, all natives of the Virgin Islands were granted citizenship and, in 1936, steps toward complete self-government began. All residents over twenty-one who could read and write English were given the right to vote.

Many U.S. servicemen were introduced to St. Croix during World War II. They trained to be fighter pilots at Benedict Field, an army air corps base on Negro Bay. St. Croix gained an airfield, which was turned over for civilian use after the war. One negative

A U.S. fort in the Virgin Islands in 1940

result of constructing the airfield was the destruction of some fine historic estate buildings surrounding it.

## Preserving the Past

After the war, a few people from the mainland United States moved to Christiansted. Some of them bought and restored old buildings to live in. A few local residents were encouraged by this interest in preservation. Along with some of the newcomers, they founded an association that is still active more than fifty years later. The St. Croix Landmarks League has done a great deal to protect the historic legacy of the Virgin Islands.

One of the league's first challenges was to protect historic public buildings in Christiansted. In 1952, a 7-acre (3-ha) area on the waterfront was put in the care of the National Park Service. The Christiansted National Historic Site includes the Customs House, the Steeple Building, and other eighteen- and nineteenth-century structures. Whim Greathouse, once the heart of a huge sugarcane plantation, showcases the league's preservation efforts. The lifestyle of colonial days in the Caribbean is explained and illustrated in exhibits and guided tours. The league also conducts annual house tours and antiques auctions, and is involved in research and educational projects related to island history.

Another nonprofit organization, the Committee to Revive Our Culture (CROC), operates a store where locally produced items are sold. The CROC also presents demonstrations and talks in schools and holds two cultural fairs each year.

The governor's house on Christiansted has been preserved as a historic public building.

# CHAPTER EIGHT

# U.S. Virgin Islands: The Land, Sea, and Living Things

About sixty or seventy islands make up the U.S. Virgin Islands. None of these islands is very large, and some are quite tiny. The largest are St. Croix, St. Thomas, St. John, and Water Islands. Most often, only the first three are talked about, but Water Island has recently been added to the list of "major" Virgin Islands. Lying at the edge of Charlotte Amalie's harbor, Water Island is increasing in popularity as a place to live.

St. Croix, with an area of 80 square miles (207 sq km), is the largest; St. Thomas covers 27 square miles (70 sq km); and St. John has 19 square miles (49 sq km)—making it slightly smaller than New York's Manhattan. Water Island has an area of only 450 acres (182 ha). Located 1,000 miles (1,609 km) south of Florida, the Vir-

The beauty of St. John attracts boaters and many other visitors.

Opposite: The Great Bay at Bluebeard's Beach

U.S. Virgin Islands
topography

gins are in the Caribbean Sea. The Atlantic Ocean laps at their northern shores. Their nearest neighbors to the east are the British Virgin Islands. Puerto Rico lies about 40 miles (64 km) to the west.

The Virgin Islands were created by volcanic action. The land is hilly with thin, rocky soil. Very few rivers or streams flow down the slope, so freshwater is in short supply. Large cisterns are used to collect rainwater.

The waters surrounding the islands are incredibly beautiful,

| U.S. Virgin Islands' Geographical Features | |
|---|---|
| **Total area** | 171 sq. mi. (443 sq km) |
| **Land** | 134 sq. mi. (347 sq km) |
| **Highest point** | Crown Mountain, St. Thomas, 1,556 feet (475 m) |
| **Lowest point** | Sea level at the Pacific Ocean |
| **Largest city** | Charlotte Amalie |
| **Population** | 119,827 (estimate) |
| **Average temperatures** | 70°F to 90°F (21°C to 32°C) |
| **Average annual rainfall** | 40 to 60 inches (102 to 152 cm) |

ranging in color from pale aquamarine in the early morning mist to a foreboding steel blue when storm clouds fill the sky. At other times, the sea is full of constantly changing blue and blue-green tints—azure, turquoise, peacock, teal, sapphire. A deep trench in the sea between St. John and St. Croix is more than 12,000 feet (3,660 m) deep.

Temperatures are mild to warm all year round, averaging 78° Fahrenheit (26° Celsius). Humidity during rainy seasons can make the atmosphere oppressive, but the rains are usually short, and ocean breezes provide relief.

## "America's Paradise"

The official nickname of the U.S. Virgin Islands is "America's Paradise." The name is printed on license plates and is used by enthusiastic observers to describe the natural wonders of these tropical islands. The mountains and beaches; the exotic birds, animals, and plants; the underwater coral gardens, the balmy air, and sunshine—all suggest a place that has been created for pleasure.

## Hurricanes

The Caribbean islands have an almost ideal climate except— and it's an important exception—when a hurricane blows through. This part of the world gets more than its share of these destructive storms.

A hurricane is a massive storm with winds that whirl in a circular formation around its center, called the "eye." In tropical regions of the North Atlantic Ocean, storms develop in low-pressure zones. They often start off the coast of North Africa and move westward. If winds reach a speed of 39 miles (63 km) per hour, the storm is classified as a cyclone, or tropical storm. At 74 miles (119 km) per hour, it is classified as a hurricane.

In recent years, the U.S. Weather Bureau has given names to the storms that threaten to come ashore in the United States. Each year, the names are selected alphabetically. For example, the first storm of the year might be called Anna, the second Bobby, and so on.

The Virgin Islands are at risk from hurricanes from June through November. July through September are considered the most dangerous months. Church services are held on July 25, Supplication Day, and people gather to pray for protection against hurricanes. Worshipers often gather again in late October for a Hurricane Thanksgiving if the weather has not been severe that season.

After about fifty years of comparative freedom from damaging hurricanes, Hurricane Hugo, in September 1989, was a major disaster. All the Virgin Islands were affected, and total damages exceeded $400 million. The losses were greatest on St. Croix, where several people were killed and 70 percent of the buildings were either destroyed or badly damaged. Hurricane Marilyn, in 1995, was most severe on St. Thomas and St. John. Damage to the islands was estimated at more than $1 billion.

In November 1999, Hurricane Lenny traveled across the islands from west to east. This is not the usual path, so the storm was nicknamed Wrong-Way Lenny. St. Croix was hit hardest and damage to the beaches was severe. ■

## Plant Life

Hundreds of varieties of tropical trees, shrubs, vines, and other plants flourish in the beautiful Virgin Islands. Flowering trees decorate the landscape with their brilliant colors. The frangipani, with its hairy leaves and white, pink, and yellow blossoms, is native to the region. The flamboyant royal poinciana tree has a profusion of brilliant orange-red blossoms throughout the summer. This tree is a native of Madagascar. Another decorative tree with bright orange-red blossoms is the African tulip from tropical West Africa.

The frangipani flower may have white, pink, and yellow blossoms.

Breadfruits grow on trees throughout the islands.

The official territorial flower is a blossom of the yellow elder, or yellow cedar, tree. The flowers are yellow and have a sweet, jam-like scent. Bees love these flowers.

Tropical fruit trees growing on the islands include the guava, lime, mango, and breadfruit. The fragrant fiddlewood tree is used to make musical instruments—including fiddles. Slaves made furniture from the wood of the genip tree. The kapok, or silk cotton, tree produces a fiber used in life preservers and sleeping bags. The calabash, the fruit of the calabash tree, is gourd-shaped. Calabashes are widely used as cups and bowls.

Mangrove trees are very important along seashores. They thrive in saltwater and put down hundreds of roots, like stilts, from their

## Weed Women

Certain female slaves on colonial plantations were known as "weed women" because they knew a great deal about the medicinal properties of various plants. They were the only medical practitioners available for most islanders.

Today, the use of natural and herbal remedies—"bush medicine"—is still accepted by many people. There are said to be some 200 medicinal plants in the Virgin Islands. Leaves of the painkiller tree, when heated and pressed against aching or swollen joints, lessen pain. The aloe plant is popular here, and throughout much of the world, to soothe the pain of cuts and burns. Congo root—also called Strong Man Bush—is used to treat stomach upsets. Tea made from haiti-haiti blossoms (seaside hibiscus) is good for colds. Lemongrass tea breaks a fever.

Weed women also knew which plants are dangerous. One of the most toxic is the manchineel tree. People should avoid all contact with this tree—even the sap is poisonous. ■

branches. This jumble of roots traps silt and decaying vegetation, eventually forming land. A mangrove thicket protects the shoreline from erosion and serves as a habitat for many forms of marine life. Mangrove trees also provide nesting areas for herons, egrets, and hummingbirds.

Several plants are known locally by colorful nicknames. Young people like to write the name of a special person on the leaf of a "love plant." A plant that sticks to anything it touches is called the "catch and keep" plant. A fast-growing bush is the "quick-stick." The "sensitive plant" curls up when it is touched. The sandbox tree's thorny trunk has given it a descriptive name: the "monkey don't climb" tree. And one tree produces "nothing nuts," so named because they are good for nothing. Various kinds of cacti and dozens of species of orchids are also found in the Virgin Islands.

At the St. George Village Botanical Garden on St. Croix, a trail leads past trees and plants marked with identification labels. The garden has a nursery, orchid house, tropical orchard, cactus area, fern house, and the ruins of a few plantation structures.

## Birds, Mammals, and Reptiles

More than 200 species of birds have been spotted on the islands. They include parakeets, pelicans, egrets, hawks, doves, sparrows, thrushes, canaries, and hummingbirds. Also, migrating shorebirds stop here on their annual journeys. The official territorial bird is the yellow breast, or banana quit.

No large mammals are native to the Virgin Islands. Several species of bats are island creatures, but mongooses, donkeys, sheep, cows, and pigs that roam freely were all introduced to the islands by people. There are also iguanas and small lizards.

A variety of flowers grow at the St. George Village Botanical Garden.

A humpback whale off the coast of St. John

## Marine Life

Fish in the Caribbean waters range from the tiny, brightly colored tropical fish prized by aquarium buffs to delicious food fish and the huge game fish sought by deep-sea fishers. Charter boats take fishers out to sea from many points on the islands.

Humpback whales migrate every year through the channel between Puerto Rico and the Virgin Islands. The whales are often spotted from December through May. Sometimes, they put on quite a show for viewers, leaping from the water, somersaulting, and diving back below the surface with loud splashes. Often, they also provide an audio portion of the show—moaning, crying, and grunting. These loud sounds are probably a form of communication, but scientists have not been able to translate them.

Both tourists and residents love to watch the sea turtles that often swim into view. Hawksbill, loggerhead, leatherback, and green turtles frequent the islands' waters. Sometimes, they appear in large groups.

## Coral Reefs

In many parts of the world, beautiful formations that look like porous, multicolored rocks are found under the sea. They are created by millions of tiny animals called polyps. Polyps feed on plankton—other tiny sea creatures and plants. When polyps die, their skeletons pile up in wonderful shapes that some geologists call "honorary rocks." We call them coral.

Coral is hard, like rock, but fragile and easily broken. Some corals look like shrubs; others resemble horns, mushrooms, even lace. Ocean currents push the coral around and pile it up. Eventually, some massive collections of coral reach above the water surface. These are actually small islands. Ring-shaped coral islands lodge on top of submerged ridges or volcanoes.

The coral reefs found near tropical shorelines are platforms of living polyps. Many of them are found in Caribbean waters. They create underwater gardens, colored green, white, purple, yellow, pink, and tan. Fish and other marine creatures, such as sea anemones and mollusks, live and move about in these coral gardens.

Buck Island Reef National Monument was established to protect the fragile coral reef and the creatures who inhabit it. It is only a short boat ride from downtown Christiansted. Snorkelers and scuba divers can get a close-up view of this ever-changing, magical, underwater world. ■

**U.S. Virgin Islands Parks**

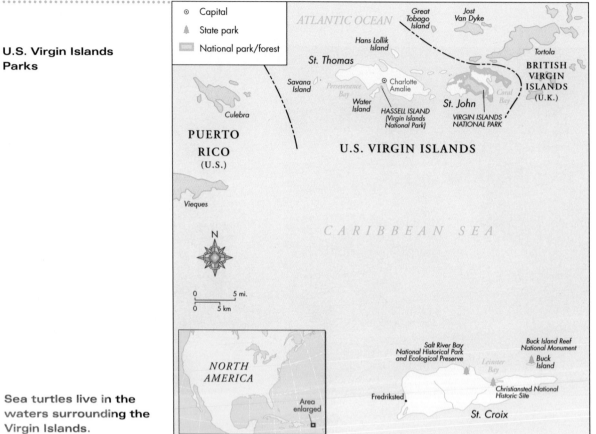

**Sea turtles live in the waters surrounding the Virgin Islands.**

Leatherback turtles are the largest, weighing as much as 1,500 pounds (681 kilograms). These giants can swim for miles and dive hundreds of feet below the surface. They have been known to travel as far as 3,000 miles (4,827 km) to lay their eggs at the place of their birth.

The region of Sandy Point, on St. Croix, is a National Wildlife Refuge established in 1978 for the protection of the turtles. It is illegal to disturb the turtles or their eggs in any way.

## Virgin Islands National Park

The Virgin Islands National Park consists of 9,039 acres (3,660 ha) of land on St. John Island surrounded by 5,650 acres (2,288 ha) of water. Much of its beauty lies underwater, where sea grasses wave and a unique coral reef thrives. A self-guided snorkeling trail is marked by underwater signs that tell viewers about the vegetation, the reef, and tropical marine life.

Experienced scuba divers can go deeper beneath the surface. Snuba is a new method that falls between snorkeling and scuba diving. The divers are attached to a tank on a raft so they can go down several feet without carrying a tank of air.

Beautiful beaches line the water's edge. Herons, pelicans, and other shorebirds hover nearby. Crabs skitter along the sand. Schools of fish glide through the water searching for their meals. Sea turtles occasionally come on shore to dig nests and lay eggs.

Ranger-guided walks on land give visitors an excellent orientation and knowledge of the history and environment of St. John Island.

The U.S. Congress authorized the park in 1956. Philanthropist and conservationist Laurance Rockefeller and his associates donated much of the land. The United Nations Educational, Scientific and Cultural Organization (UNESCO) has recognized the unique ecological value of this park by designating it a Biosphere Reserve. ■

# U.S. Virgin Islands: Government, Economy, Tourism

he Stars and Stripes were raised over the islands on March 31, 1917. The former Danish islands were officially renamed the Virgin Islands of the United States. The people of the island were happy, assuming they were now citizens of a democracy.

Actually, that wasn't the case. Legally, the U.S. Virgin Islands was—and still is—an "unincorporated territory." And, at first, the people were not U.S. citizens and had no say in their government. Officers of the U.S. Navy were in charge.

A street in the Virgin Islands, 1940s

Economic conditions in the islands were deplorable. Poverty was widespread, and the death rate was high. Many diseases were common, and there were few facilities to care for the sick. Schools and roads were almost nonexistent. In the first place in the Western Hemisphere to abolish slavery, the people were not much better off than their enslaved ancestors had been. No one was taking any responsibility for helping those in need.

The head of state for the new territory was the president of the United States. Administration was in the hands of the U.S. Navy. The first few governors of the Virgin Islands were military officers who believed in authoritarian rule. Many officers were also white

Opposite: Sailing in St. John

## The Territorial Flag and Seal

The flag of the United States Virgin Islands was adopted in 1917. A yellow American eagle with the shield of the United States on its breast is centered on a white background. It clutches a sprig of laurel in one talon and a bundle of three blue arrows in the other. The letter *V* is on one side of the eagle; *I* is on the other.

The great seal of the Virgin Islands was adopted by the territorial legislature in 1990. The yellow breast (*Coreba flaveola*), the territorial bird, sits on a branch of the yellow cedar (*Tecoma stans*), the territorial flower. There are three blossoms and three seed pods on the branch, and three islands are in the background around the bird. The number three symbolizes the three major islands of the territory. On one of the islands, representing St. Croix, is a sugar mill. The Annaberg ruins are pictured on the island representing St. John, and the flags of the United States of America and Dannebrog are on the island representing St. Thomas. At the bottom is a scroll inscribed "United in Pride and Hope." A circular border contains the words "Government of the United States Virgin Islands." ■

supremacists, who had little knowledge of, or respect for, people of color.

Over the years, the governmental structure gradually changed. Most Virgin Islanders were granted U.S. citizenship in 1927. In 1931, the administration was transferred from the navy to the Department of Interior, and a civilian governor was appointed. The following year, citizenship was extended to all adults who could read and write English.

## The Government Today

President Franklin D. Roosevelt became the thirty-second president of the United States in 1933. He was a distant cousin of Theodore Roosevelt, who had gained fame—and later the presidency—during the Spanish-American War. At that time, the nation and most of the world were in the depths of the Great Depression, and President Roosevelt established a number of programs to stimulate the economy and help the poor. One of his New Deal programs, as they were called, was the Public Works Administration. This government agency set up a public corporation in the Virgin Islands to manufacture rum.

A government building in St. Thomas

President Roosevelt signed the Organic Act in 1936, which stated, among other things, that the U.S. Constitution would apply to the Virgin Islands. The act included a bill of rights and prohibited discrimination on the basis of race, color, sex, or religious belief. Citizens would have the right to vote for a local government, which would consist of two municipal councils and a legislative assembly. All federal taxes collected in the islands would be held for use by the local government.

## U.S. Virgin Islands Official Song
## "The Virgin Islands March"

Music by Alton A. Adams

*All hail our Virgin Islands.*
*Em'ralds of the sea,*
*Where beaches bright with*
*    coral sand*
*And trade winds bless our*
*    native land.*
*All hail our Virgin Islands,*
*Bathed in waters blue,*
*We give our loyalty,*
*Full to thee,*
*And pledge allegiance forever*
*    true.*

*To thee our Virgin Islands,*
*Loving voices raise*
*A song in praise of brother-*
*    hood,*

*Where right makes might to*
*    fight for good.*
*To thee our Virgin Islands,*
*Haven of the free,*
*We sing our love to thee,*
*Joyously,*
*Our own fair islands of liberty.*

*March on oh Virgin Islands,*
*In the joyful throng,*
*Uphold the right and right the*
*    wrong*
*Where only peace and love*
*    belong.*
*March on oh Virgin Islands,*
*Democratic land.*
*Together hand in hand,*

*Take your stand,*
*Forever soldiers in freedom's*
*    band.*

*God bless our Virgin Islands,*
*Humbly now we pray,*
*Where all mankind can join*
*    today*
*In friendly warmth of work and*
*    play.*
*God bless our Virgin Islands,*
*Beautiful and tall.*
*Beneath a sunny sky,*
*Hilltops high*
*Hold out a welcome for one*
*    and all.*

The Virgin Islanders elected their first legislature in 1954. Governors continued to be appointed by the U.S. president until 1970. The first black governor was appointed in 1946. In 1958, the appointed governor was the first native-born islander to hold that office.

The islanders elected their own governor for the first time in 1970. The governor, elected by the people, serves for four years. The legislature has one house, consisting of fifteen senators who serve two-year terms. Local courts handle judicial matters. Citizens cannot vote in presidential elections while living on the islands, but they send a nonvoting delegate to sit in the U.S. House of Representatives.

## Territorial Symbols

The yellow breast (*Coreba flaveola*) (left) was named the official bird of the territory by the legislature in 1970. Also called the sugar bird or banana quit, the bird has brilliant yellow plumage. Native to the islands, it is plentiful, friendly, and known for its taste for sugar.

The blossom of the yellow elder, or yellow cedar, tree was proclaimed the official territorial flower in 1934. It blooms all year round and is native to the Virgin Islands. ▪

The territory has not yet enacted a constitution. Several drafts were proposed during the 1980s and 1990s, but each one failed to be accepted by the Congress or the electorate—or both.

The islanders are not completely satisfied with the current state of political affairs. Some would like to become an independent nation, others hope for eventual statehood. Neither faction has enough support to win at this point.

## The Island Economy

Lovely white beaches, gem-colored waters, spectacular scenery both on land and underwater, and ideal sailing weather much of the time are among the blessings of the Virgin Islands. As for other natural resources, there are no minerals to speak of, except stone. The

**Enjoying a day at the beach**

land is rocky and thin, not worth much as farmland. Agriculture is not an important part of the economy. A few small farmers raise most of the food for their own families, but hardly any for sale.

Residents of the islands depend heavily on imported foods. Even the sugar used in the processing of Virgin Islands rum is imported. Sugar production, once the island's main industry, is no longer a profitable enterprise.

Freshwater is scarce on the islands, so plants have been built to desalinize (remove the salt from) water from the sea. These installations generate electric power and produce freshwater. This provides some light industry. The Virgin Islands' leaders are still seeking ways to attract more income-producing industries.

U.S. Virgin Islands
resources

## What the U.S. Virgin Islands Grows, Manufactures, and Mines

| Agriculture | Manufacturing | Mining |
|---|---|---|
| Beef cattle | Alumina | Gravel |
| Chickens | Concrete products | Sand |
| Eggs | Petroleum products | |
| Goats | Rum | |
| Hogs | Textiles | |
| Milk | Watches | |
| Vegetables | | |

## Eco-tourism

Thousands of people want to visit beautiful places like the Virgin Islands. They hope to see unspoiled lands, breathe pure air, swim in clean waters, and stroll through uncrowded green places. But the more the people visit these places, the more their natural beauty is threatened.

Until a few years ago, many people had never even heard the word *ecology*—the study of the relationships among all living things and their environment. Recently, however, ecology has become a popular. Scientists remind us of the dangers of using up the natural resources that cannot be replaced. They tell us that numerous species of plants and animals are in danger of extinction. They warn of possible worldwide disaster caused by global warming.

A new kind of travel has grown out of these concerns. It has several names—eco-tourism, green travel, responsible tourism. The common thread is that people should travel to learn about different environments, but they should do everything possible not to disturb or alter the ecosystems and

**Taking an eco-tour of a St. Croix rain forest**

cultures they visit. Several nonprofit organizations—such as the Audubon Society and the Nature Conservancy—conduct "eco-tours" in the Virgin Islands. They stress such activities as hiking, biking, diving, bird-watching, and whale-watching.

Maho Bay Camps and Harmony Studios, on the north side of St. John, are resorts designed to accommodate visitors in comfort while doing the least possible damage to the environment. Guests at Maho Bay stay in "tent-cottages," built on wooden floors supported by stilts and connected by wooden boardwalks, so the vegetation is not disturbed by people tramping over it. This protects the soil from the erosion that endangers the beach and coral.

Walls on three sides of the cottages are actually screens, giving visitors an unobstructed view of the waters and woods around them. Each cottage has a deck. Cooking facilities consist of a camp stove and portable cooler.

Two other resorts built more recently are Estate Concordia Studios and Concordia Eco-tents. These were designed with the same philosophy, to combine environmental concern with comfort. In every possible case, recycled materials were used in construction. Solar generators provide electricity, and water is recycled. ◼

Guests stay in "tent-cottages" at Maho Bay.

Tourism is the most important segment of the U.S. Virgin Islands economy. Air service to the islands is good—airfields constructed by the military during World War II are now used for commercial and private air travel. Large hotels and resorts have been built to accommodate visitors. Tourism produces a snowball effect, attracting many new businesses, such as restaurants, local transportation, shops, and other services.

Most visitors to the islands, however, arrive on cruise ships or private boats. They dock at Frederiksted and Christiansted on St. Croix and Charlotte Amalie and Crown Bay on St. Thomas.

**Cruise ships in the St. Thomas harbor**

An average of more than 100 cruise ships per month dock at the harbors of these islands. Some of them are huge—towering many stories high and carrying more passengers than most hotels can accommodate. (Only smaller ships can stop at Christiansted.) Crowds of passengers come on shore, anxious to sightsee, shop, or sample local foods. All these activities generate millions of dollars for local businesses.

A shopping mall is the first thing cruise passengers see as they disembark in Charlotte Amalie. Cabs and local tour operators eagerly greet the newcomers, offering to show them the local

**Tourists have fun shopping and dining in Charlotte Amalie.**

sights. Frederiksted, which is quiet—almost a ghost town—on other days, teems with life when the ships come in. The main street is lined with vendors' stalls, and street entertainers appear. If the ships are not leaving until late evening, the atmosphere becomes one of a mini-carnival.

Some of the visitors enjoy active sports, such as snorkeling, diving, and hiking. The national park areas on St. John and Buck Islands are major attractions for nature lovers.

# CHAPTER TEN

# U.S. Virgin Islands Culture

**P**eople lived on these islands many hundreds of years ago. We know very little about them because none of their descendants are here today. The Native Americans of the Virgin Islands may have migrated from Central and South America. Archaeologists have found evidence of a 1,000-year-old village that shows some similarities to Mayan and Aztec settlements. When Europeans settled here, along with the African slaves they brought in, the native population rapidly disappeared. Most of them probably died from exposure to new diseases or were starved out by the newcomers.

Many people in the Virgin Islands are descendants of Africans and Europeans.

## The People

Virgin Islanders are descended from a variety of ethnic groups, mostly from Africa and Europe. The Africans were brought here by

Opposite: A girl in St. Croix

## Laurance Rockefeller

When Laurance Rockefeller, one of the five sons of John D. Rockefeller Jr., first visited the island of St. John in the 1950s, he called it "the most beautiful island in the Caribbean." He immediately decided that much of it should be preserved in a national park. He set about buying large parcels of land, then donated 5,000 acres (2,025 ha)

to the U.S. government. People had been discussing this idea for many years, and Rockefeller's gift was the spur that Congress needed. The Virgin Islands National Park was established in 1956.

Conservation owes a great deal to the wealthy Rockefeller family. John D. Rockefeller Jr. inherited great wealth, and he believed in using it to help make the world better. He loved the outdoors, and taught his sons to love and protect the natural beauty of wilderness areas.

Over many years, John D. Rockefeller Jr. and his sons donated land and contributed millions of dollars to establish and improve national parks. In this way, all Americans have

inherited a bit of his wealth. They enjoy that inheritance whenever they visit Acadia National Park in Maine, Grand Teton in Wyoming, Shenandoah in Virginia, Mammoth Cave in Kentucky, and the Great Smoky Mountains in North Carolina and Tennessee.

Throughout his long life, Laurance Rockefeller has continued to help the cause of conservation in many ways. The American Conservation Association and the World Wildlife Fund are just two of a long list of organizations he has assisted. In 1990, President George H. W. Bush presented a gold medal to Laurance Rockefeller in recognition of his lifetime contributions to parks and recreation. ■

force and enslaved by the Europeans, but the West Indian culture owes as much to Africa as it does to Europe.

Europeans were slow in settling the Virgin Islands. More than 100 years passed after Columbus spotted the islands before the first European settlers moved in. By the 1630s, English, Dutch, and French settlers were living on Santa Cruz, as the Spanish called St. Croix. Danish colonizers began to develop the land around the harbor on St. Thomas in 1666.

Present-day islanders who are descended from old European families have names that reflect their varying heritage—English,

French, Danish, Dutch, Irish, and Scottish. There were small neighborhoods of Jews, both Sephardic and Ashkenazi, before the American Revolution. The Danish West Indies had a Jewish governor for two years, appointed by King Christian VI of Denmark in 1734.

Some residents are people from the U.S. mainland who visited the islands, fell in love with them, and returned to establish year-round or vacation homes.

**A basket weaver in St. John**

Immigrants from other Caribbean islands have also added to the variety of European ethnic groups on the U.S. Virgin Islands. Farmers and fishers from the French islands of Saint-Barthélemy (St. Barts) and St. Christopher (St. Kitts) came to St. Thomas in the 1800s. A community near the harbor in Charlotte Amalie, still called Frenchtown, was originally a fishing village. One street retains its French name, Rue de St. Barthélemy. Residents celebrate French Heritage Week each year. They wear traditional French costumes and fill the air with the rousing sounds of the French national anthem, "La Marseillaise."

Puerto Ricans have been here, especially on St. Croix, since the earliest Danish settlements. Even after several generations, many of their descendants still speak Spanish at home.

The twentieth century brought even more variety to the Virgin Islands. A number of Dominicans migrated from Hispaniola, the island shared by Haiti and the Dominican Republic. Many of them became proprietors of small businesses. A few Arabs—both Muslims and Christians—and some East Indians are in business and in the professions in the U.S. Virgins. Some came from Asia, and some came by way of other Caribbean islands.

## Religion

The Frederick Evangelical Lutheran Church was built in 1826.

The island of St. Croix has 166 churches. Protestants of many different denominations are the largest religious group in the Virgin Islands, but Roman Catholics have more members than any single Protestant sect.

Danish colonists established a Lutheran congregation on St. Thomas in 1666. The Frederick Evangelical Lutheran Church, still in use, was built in 1826, using bricks from earlier churches. Other Lutheran congregations were soon organized on St. Croix and St. Thomas. All Saints Anglican (Episcopal) Church in St. Thomas was built in 1848 and dedicated "to the glory of God in thanksgiving for freedom from slavery." Moravian missionaries, such as Friederich Martin, who was called the Apostle to the Negroes, worked to convert the slaves to Christianity. Bethany Moravian Church on St. John dates from 1754. Other Protestant denominations on the islands today include Baptist, Methodist, Seventh-day Adventist, and several Evangelicals.

One of the oldest Jewish congregations in the Western Hemisphere was established in Charlotte Amalie. The original Synagogue of Bracha V'Shalom V'Gemilut Chasidim was originally constructed in 1796 and rebuilt in 1833.

This synagogue was constructed in 1796.

Both Jews and Catholics worshiped in private in early years, overshadowed by a Protestant majority. Like the Moravians, Catholics recruited converts among blacks. Catholic churches were built on St. Croix and St. Thomas in the early 1800s.

The close-knit East Indian community is composed largely of Hindus. East Indian shops display small Hindu shrines and pictures of Hindu deities. Diwali, the Hindu festival of lights, is celebrated annually. There is also an Islamic mosque on St. Croix. The most important Muslim observance is the holy month of Ramadan.

Quite a few Caribbean people of African descent are devotees of a fairly new religion called Rastafarianism. The emperor of Ethiopia, Haile Selassie, also known as Ras Tafari, was crowned in 1930. Many blacks around the world saw him as the savior of their people, the one prophesied in the Bible and in the writings of Marcus Garvey, a black Jamaican leader. Rastafarian sects developed in Jamaica and spread to other islands. Most Rastas (the name for the brethren) eat a vegetarian diet and live simply.

Boating and diving are favorite activities in the Virgin Islands.

## Everyday Life

People in the U.S. Virgin Islands live much as folks on the mainland do. Children go to school; adults go to work. Because many mothers have jobs, many young children go to day-care centers after school. Older children enjoy a variety of after-school activities, such as volleyball, baseball, and soccer.

One big difference between life in the islands and life on much of mainland America is that no one in the Virgin Islands needs to buy overcoats or boots, and homes don't need central heating. It never snows or gets really cold.

Another difference is that beaches are always nearby. Families spend a lot of time at the beach, or fishing, on weekends. Line fishing is popular. Fishers don't use poles. They just hold the string in their hands. It takes practice to catch fish this way.

Island men love to play dominoes. On any Sunday afternoon, several hotly contested domino games are going on in the parks.

St. Croix residents call themselves Crucians. The other islanders are St. Thomians or St. Johnians. Ferries carry people—and cars, if needed—back and forth between St. Thomas and St. John. When St. John children finish elementary school, they commute to the high school on St. Thomas by ferry.

There's not as much everyday travel between St. Croix and the other islands. The distance is much greater, and the only transportation is by private boat or on regularly scheduled seaplane flights. The flights are too costly for frequent travel, except for business trips.

## Food

Agriculture is not an important part of the economy of the Virgin
Islands, and most food is imported. Farmers grow fruits and vegetables and raise a few domestic animals for meat, but these are
mostly for their own families.

In spite of this shortage of local food products—or perhaps
because of it—Virgin Island cuisine includes delicious specialties
from many cultures.

Virgin Island food is
often made from fruits
and seafood.

The Caribbean waters pro-
vide a wonderful variety of fish
and other seafood. Popular,
large, deep-sea fish are marlin,
tuna, and mahi mahi. These, as
well as snapper and grouper,
are often served with a
coconut-cream sauce. Conch,
crab, spiny lobster, and shrimp
are baked and grilled and used
in salads and chowders.

## Language

The language spoken in the U.S. Virgins is English, but with a strong Caribbean accent and a mixture of local words and phrases. Sometimes this speech is called Creole, or "English with a calypso beat." As one newcomer to the islands put it, "There's English in there, but sometimes you have to listen hard to hear it."

Because so many people have come here from other islands, the language has a variety of accents and vocabulary. A bit of Spanish often creeps in, along with a mixture of Dutch, Danish, French, and African sayings. Names of streets and neighborhoods often have Danish endings.

Common words and phrases heard in the U.S. Virgin Islands include the following:

| | |
|---|---|
| cheese-an-bread! | an expression of surprise |
| cuno-muno | peculiar person, an oddball |
| gut | small stream or dry streambed |
| jumbi | ghost or spirit |
| mash-up | accident |
| melee | gossip |
| midge | tiny bug, sand fly |
| mocko jumbi | masked stilt walker |
| pistarckle | confusion, stupidity |
| rubbyhux | a rough person |
| salting | a main dish of meat or fish |
| sugarcake | candy |

Tropical fruits, such as soursop, sweetsop, papaya, mango, guava, sorrel, passion fruit, and pineapple are used in drinks and exotic desserts or simply eaten fresh. Grated coconut adds a delightful flavor to cakes and tarts.

Some of the foods associated with the Caribbean, such as yams, akee, and red peas, were brought by African slaves. The Spanish brought bananas and plantains across the ocean from the

## Pumpkin Soup

This delicious soup is often found in the Virgin Islands, where it's a great warm-weather treat.

### Ingredients:

1 16-ounce can of pumpkin
4 cups of chicken broth
2 cups of half-and-half
1 large onion, sliced
3/4 cups of scallion, sliced, white part only
1/4 cups of butter
1 bay leaf
1/2 teaspoon sugar
1/2 teaspoon curry powder
1/8 teaspoon nutmeg
1 tablespoon of dry parsley
2 teaspoons salt
ground pepper

### Directions:

Saute the onion in butter until light brown. Stir in the pumpkin, chicken broth, bay leaf, sugar, curry powder, nutmeg, and dry parsley. Simmer uncovered for 15 minutes, stirring occasionally.

Stir in the half-and-half slowly. Add salt, then pepper to taste. Simmer for an additional 5 to 10 minutes.

Canary Islands. Later immigrants introduced savory and fiery spices. A favorite snack food is pate, a fried pastry turnover filled with a mixture of meat or seafood, vegetables, and spices.

Special occasions demand special foods. To celebrate Transfer Day, March 31 (when the United States took over ownership of the islands), the traditional foods combine Danish and Caribbean dishes. Included are a fruit dish called red grout, marinated herring snacks, and almond cake.

Every St. Croix cook has a personal recipe for callaloo—a dish served on New Year's Eve. Originally made from the bone of the Christmas ham boiled with greens and seasonings, today it often includes bits of seafood and fish. Black cake, always expected at wedding celebrations, is a very rich concoction of fruits, nuts, spices, liqueurs, and sugar.

Carnival celebrations include a food fair. Local cooks offer their best products—candies, cookies, and dozens of other delicacies—at these festivals.

## Music and Dance

Reggae is a popular style of music in the Virgin Islands.

Extemporaneous lyrics set to joyous melodies and punctuated with a vigorous beat—that's the essence of Caribbean music. Reggae and rap are today's favorites in the Virgin Islands, but they are only two forms out of a vast musical repertoire. Today's Caribbean music has spread from Africa and Europe through Latin America, Trinidad, Jamaica, Puerto Rico, and other islands.

Slaves carried their musical traditions in their hearts as they left Africa. They used music to share their thoughts with others and ease their endless hours of backbreaking toil. Cariso songs ("carry it like so") were a form of communication for people who were not allowed to meet in gatherings or visit other plantations. Cariso lyrics were sung to the accompaniment of homemade congas, maracas, and other percussion instruments.

Quelbe lyrics discusses all kinds of current events—private gossip as well as social comment. Quelbe bands use one or more wind instruments—flute, clarinet, or saxophone—plus strings—guitar, ukelele, or banjo.

All these musical forms have African origins, like calypso, which first developed and became popular in Trinidad. Lyrics for calypso songs are often improvised by the singers. Contemporary reggae and rap forms follow the improvisational tradition.

Over the years, slaves on the plantations learned some of their owners' European musical forms. Hymns sung in European churches, stately ballroom dance music such as the waltz, and lively European folk tunes such as polkas and reels became intermingled with African forms. These traditions evolved into what is now Caribbean music.

A type of musical group popular in the islands is the "scratch," or fungi band. Players add unique sounds to the music of traditional instruments by scratching on the sides of gourds with wire combs and using washtubs, pipes, and bottles as drums.

The twentieth century brought a new sound to Caribbean music. During World War II, street musicians in Trinidad used steel oil drums salvaged from U.S. military bases to create the steel pan. They sliced off the top sections of the oil drums and pounded out small, rounded sections something like those in a divided paper plate. When pounded, each section produces a different note of the scale. Steel drum bands became wildly popular almost overnight, and the sounds of the Caribbean islands echoed around the world.

## Festivals

Carnivals in the Virgin Islands, as in other Caribbean countries, have a dual heritage. The Spanish colonials brought a tradition of celebrating just before Lent. During Lent, devout Catholics abstained from eating meat. The word *carnival* actually comes from two Latin words, *carne vale*, meaning "farewell to meat." The West African slaves had a tradition of masquerade parties, with music, dancing, and partying in the streets. These two backgrounds merge in the Caribbean Carnival.

On St. Thomas, Carnival is held some time after Easter. All kinds of competitions, lots of calypso music, street entertainers, steel drum bands, parades, amusement-park rides, horse races, arts and crafts displays, and food booths featuring favorite local dishes are part of the fun. But the parades are the main attraction. Hundreds of people take part, dressed in imaginative, brilliantly colored costumes. They dance, march to band music, and perform on elaborate floats. The celebration is climaxed with a dazzling fireworks display.

St. John celebrates Carnival, along with U.S. Independence Day, on the Fourth of July. It's not as big and boisterous as the one on St.

A steel drum band performing at a St. John festival

## Mocko Jumbies

Mocko jumbies are the Virgin Islanders' favorite street entertainers, and no big celebration is complete without them. They tower over the marchers and floats in parades, stealing the stage wherever they go.

Jumbies are ghosts and spirits—supernatural figures in the legend and lore of the Caribbean. Mocko jumbies are performers who appear to have supernatural powers because they are walking—and even dancing—on tall stilts.

Because of their height, they are a symbol of protection from evil for the people and villages they tower over. Their masks and costumes are designed to scare away all forms of danger.

Some Virgin Island children start to learn stilt walking at an early age, hoping to become expert. Troupes of mocko jumbies have performed all over the world, including appearances in Macy's Thanksgiving Day Parade in New York City. ■

Thomas, because St. John has fewer people. In Cruz Bay, people arrive from other ports to watch the festivities from their yachts.

Crucian Christmas Festival is the big event of the year on St. Croix. It starts before Christmas Day and lasts until Three Kings' Day (January 6). Festival Villages are set up in both Christiansted and Frederiksted. The spirit of *bambooshay*—a French word meaning "live it up"—fills the air.

St. Croix native Horace Clarke as a New York Yankee

## Sports

School sports in the U.S. Virgin Islands include baseball, volleyball, football, basketball, and soccer. Other popular spectator sports are cricket and horse racing.

The islands have produced a few homegrown sports heroes, such as Julian Jackson. Known as the Champ, he is a St. Thomas native who once held the World Boxing Association middleweight title. Several Virgin Islanders have played Major-League Baseball,

### Tim Duncan

Tim Duncan, a young St. Croix student, was an excellent swimmer who trained hard in the hope that he might someday be on an Olympic swimming team. Misfortune blew those hopes away when a violent hurricane destroyed the pool where trained. A relative suggested that the 7-foot (213 cm)-tall teenaged athlete should consider playing basketball.

Duncan went to Wake Forest College in North Carolina. When he graduated in 1997, he was the number-one draft choice of the National Basketball Association.

Today Cruzians are proud of their former neighbor and his record with the San Antonio Spurs. He was named Rookie of the Year in 1998 and the NBA Most Valuable Player in 1999. Duncan was born in 1976. His family still lives in St. Croix. ■

**A regatta in St. Thomas**

including Jerry Browne, Joe Christopher, and Horace Clark of St. Croix, and Elrod Hendricks and Alvin McBean of St. Thomas.

St. Croix hosts a Sportsweek Festival each spring, where players compete in a variety of events such as footraces, tennis tournaments, deep-sea fishing, and underwater photography.

The islands' wealth of opportunities for outdoor recreation help make tourism a major industry here. Yachts and deep-sea fishing boats are available for charter, and yacht races and regattas are popular events. The surrounding waters and undersea views are excellent for snorkeling and scuba diving. Some areas are also good for surfing and windsurfing.

On land, there are facilities for golf, tennis, and horseback riding. And hikers and campers love the islands, especially in and near Virgin Islands National Park.

## Touring the Islands

St. Croix, the largest of the U.S. Virgins, was once covered with sugarcane plantations. Today, it consists of two main towns, Christiansted and Frederiksted, which are separated by small settlements and a few resorts.

Downtown Christiansted, with its narrow streets and historic buildings, has the flavor of the eighteenth-century Danish colonial town it used to be. Several of the old structures, including Fort Christiansvaern, are part of the Christiansted National Historic Site. The wharf, once a busy center of international trade, is quiet and peaceful much of the time.

**Fort Christiansvaern**

Sailboats docked at the waterfront carry passengers on sunset cruises or trips to Buck Island Reef National Monument. Visitors to Buck Island can snorkel, explore the beach, or hike a nature trail to an overlook for an impressive view of the reef.

Whim Greathouse is the only restored sugar mill on an island which was once dotted with more than 200 mills. The furnishings of the house illustrate the luxurious lifestyle enjoyed by Danish planters. A 17-acre (7-ha) park, St. George Village Botanical Garden, stands on the ruins of an old sugar plantation. Marked trails lead visitors through collections of more than 800 species of plants.

The grounds at Whim Plantation

The pier at Coral World Marine Park

Cruise ships make frequent stops at Frederiksted's deepwater harbor. Fort Frederik, on the north side of the pier, was the spot where the governor of the Danish West Indies proclaimed freedom for all the slaves.

St. Thomas is the busiest of the islands, crowded with homes, hotels, shops, and restaurants. Sightseeing guides greet the many huge cruise ships that dock there every week, eager to show off their island to tourists. The views from the mountains are spectacular. One of the best views in the world can be seen from the top of St. Peter Mountain. It encompasses the panorama of the city, the waterfront, and the ships at anchor.

Drake's Seat on Crown Mountain is named for Sir Francis Drake—although he probably never set foot on St. Thomas. Far below is Magens Bay, a sand-fringed jewel of aquamarine water. Beyond it is Sir Francis Drake Channel, the passage between the Caribbean Sea and the Atlantic Ocean.

Coral World Marine Park has a baby shark pool, turtle pools, and a "touch pond" for kids. Several house museums and parks on St. Thomas are open to the public.

St. John is truly a nature lover's paradise, whether one wants to explore on land or in the water. The national park occupies a large

part of the island. It includes twenty-two nature trails, and park rangers lead a variety of walks to introduce visitors to the island's wealth of natural treasures.

Many consider St. John a natural paradise.

# Timeline

## United States History

The first permanent English settlement is established in North America at Jamestown. **1607**

Pilgrims found Plymouth Colony, the second permanent English settlement. **1620**

America declares its independence from Britain. **1776**

The Treaty of Paris officially ends the Revolutionary War in America. **1783**

The U.S. Constitution is written. **1787**

The Louisiana Purchase almost doubles the size of the United States. **1803**

The United States and Britain fight the War of 1812. **1812–15**

The North and South fight each other in the American Civil War. **1861–65**

## U.S. Territories History

**1521** Portuguese explorer Ferdinand Magella sights the island of Guam as he sails around the world.

**1668** Guam becomes one of the first Pacific islands settled by Europeans when Spanish missionaries arrive.

**1673** The first African slaves are brought to S Thomas to work in sugarcane plantatio

**1848** The slaves in the West Indies are eman pated on July 3.

**1867** The United States acquires Midway At the nation's first overseas possession.

**1876** After 100 years of independence, the U States expands across the continent.

**1878** Labor riots on St. Croix leads to the burning of much of the island.

**1898** The United States acquires the Philipp Puerto Rico, Wake Island, and Guam through a treaty signed on December

**1899** The United States takes control of the eastern Samoan islands.

**1901** William Howard Taft is sworn in as the American governor of the Philippines; Congress creates a two-house legislatu in Puerto Rico.

# United States History

The United States is **1917–18**
involved in World War I.

The stock market crashes, **1929**
plunging the United States into
the Great Depression.

The United States **1941–45**
fights in World War II.

The United States becomes a **1945**
charter member of the U.N.

The United States **1951–53**
fights in the Korean War.

The U.S. Congress enacts a series of **1964**
groundbreaking civil rights laws.

The United States **1964–73**
engages in the Vietnam War.

The United States and other **1991**
nations fight the brief
Persian Gulf War against Iraq.

# U.S. Territories History

**1905** The eastern Samoan islands are officially named American Samoa and the native people become U.S. nationals.

**1917** Puerto Rican citizens receive U.S. citizenship; the United States purchases St. Thomas, St. John, and St. Croix.

**1927** People living in the U.S. Virgin Islands acquire U.S. citizenship.

**1946** Congress declares the Republic of the Philippines independent on July 4.

**1947** The United Nations creates the Trust Territory of the Pacific Islands, including the Marshall, Caroline, and Mariana Islands.

**1952** The United States establishes the Commonwealth of Puerto Rico; the St. Croix National Historic Site is established.

**1962** A typhoon on Guam destroys most buildings, kills nine people, and demolishes two towns.

**1967** The constitution for American Samoa is written.

**1970** Guam holds governmental elections for the first time.

**1988** The United States establishes the National Park of American Samoa.

**1991** The Republic of the Marshall Islands becomes an independent nation, with a compact of free association with the United States; the Caroline Islands become the Federated States of Micronesia, also in free association with the United States.

**1996** Midway Atoll is declared a National Wildlife Refuge; control is transferred from the U.S. Navy to the Fish and Wildlife Service of the Department of the Interior.

# Fast Facts

Agana

## Guam

| | |
|---:|---|
| **Capital** | Agana (Hagatna) |
| **Motto** | "Where America's Day Begins" |
| **Languages** | English, Chamorro/Chamoru, Japanese |
| **Bird** | Marianas rose crown fruit dove |
| **Flower** | Bougainvillea |
| **Song** | "Guam Hymn" |
| **National holidays** | Guam Discovery Day, first Monday in March; Liberation Day, July 21 |
| **Constitution** | Organic Act of August 1950 |
| **Tree** | Ifil |

War Memorial of Guam

| | |
|---|---|
| **Total area** | 217 sq. mi. (562 sq km) |
| **Land** | 210 sq. mi. (544 sq km) |
| **Latitude and longitude** | Guam is located at 13° 28′ N and 144° 47′ E |
| **Highest point** | Mount Lamlam, Agat District, 1,332 feet (406 m) |
| **Lowest point** | Sea level at the Pacific Ocean |
| **Largest city** | Agana (Hagatna) |
| **Population** | 151,716 (estimate) |
| **Average temperatures** | 70°F to 90°F (21°C to 32°C) |
| **Average annual rainfall** | 90 inches (229 cm) |
| **Universities** | The University of Guam, established in 1952 |
| **National park** | War in the Pacific National Historic Park |

Pago Pago

## American Samoa

| | |
|---|---|
| **Capital** | Pago Pago |
| **Motto** | *Samoa Muamua le Atua* ("In Samoa, God is First") |
| **Languages** | Samoan, English |
| **Flower** | Paogo |
| **Song** | "Amerika Samoa" |
| **National holiday** | Territorial Flag Day, April 17 |
| **Constitution** | Ratified 1966, in effect 1967 |
| **Total area** | 90 sq. mi. (233 sq km) |

Village school in
American Samoa

| | |
|---|---|
| **Land** | 77 sq. mi. (199 sq km) |
| **Latitude and longitude** | American Samoa is located at 14° 20′ S and 170° 00′ W |
| **Highest point** | Lata Mountain, Tau Island, 3,160 feet (964 m) |
| **Lowest point** | Sea level at the Pacific Ocean |
| **Largest city** | Pago Pago |
| **Population** | 63,786 (estimate) |
| **Average temperatures** | 70°F to 90°F (21°C to 32°C) |
| **Average annual rainfall** | 200 inches (508 cm) |
| **National park** | National Park of American Samoa |

## Virgin Islands of the United States

Charlotte Amalie

| | |
|---|---|
| **Capital** | Charlotte Amalie |
| **Nickname** | America's Paradise |
| **Language** | English |
| **Bird** | Yellow breast |
| **Flower** | Yellow elder or yellow trumpet |
| **Song** | "The Virgin Islands March" |
| **National holiday** | Transfer Day, March 31 |
| **Constitution** | 1954 Revised Organic Act of the Virgin Islands |
| **Total area** | 171 sq. mi. (443 sq km) |
| **Land** | 134 sq. mi. (347 sq km) |

**Girl in St. Croix**

| | |
|---|---|
| **Latitude and longitude** | Virgin Islands of the United States are located at 18° 20' N and 64° 50' W |
| **Highest point** | Crown Mountain, St. Thomas, 1,556 feet (475 m) |
| **Lowest point** | Sea level at the Atlantic Ocean |
| **Largest city** | Charlotte Amalie |
| **Population** | 119,827 (estimate) |
| **Average temperatures** | 70°F to 90°F (21°C to 32°C) |
| **Average annual rainfall** | 40 to 60 inches (102 to 152 cm) |
| **College** | The College of the Virgin Islands |
| **National park** | Virgin Islands National Park |

# To Find Out More

## History

- Aylesworth, Thomas G., and Virginia L. Aylesworth. *Territories and Possessions.* New York: Chelsea House, 1988

- Kristen, Katherine, and Kathleen Thompson. *Pacific Islands.* Austin, Tex.: Raintree/Steck-Vaughn, 1996

- Martel, Arlene R. *USVI, America's Virgin Islands.* London: Macmillan Education Ltd., 1998.

## Fiction

- Medlicott, Joan A. *Virgin Islands Tales of Olden Days.* Barnardsville, N.C.: Picara Point Publisher, 1997.

- Waters, Erika J. *New Writing from the Caribbean.* London: Macmillan Education Ltd., 1994.

## American Samoa Websites

■ **American Samoa Official Website**

*http://www.government.as*

For information about American Samoa's government and people

■ **National Park of American Samoa**

*http://www.nps.gov/npsa/*

For information about this national park

■ **Amerika Samoa**

*http://ipacific.com/samoa/samoa.html*

For information about American Samoa

## Guam Websites

■ **Guam Visitors Bureau Website**

*http//:www.visitguam.org*

For information about Guam's points of interest

■ **Guam Official Website**

*http://ns.gov.gu/*

For information about Guam's government and people

## Virgin Islands of the United States Websites

■ **Virgin Islands of the United States Official Website**

*http://www.gov.vi/*

For information about the government and people of the Virgin Islands of the United States

## Addresses

■ **American Samoa Office of Tourism**

American Samoa Governor
Department of Commerce
P.O. Box 1147
Pago Pago,
American Samoa 96799

■ **Guam Visitors Bureau**

P.O. Box 3520
Agana, Guam 96910

■ **U.S. Virgin Islands Department of Tourism**

78-123 Estate Conant
P.O. Box 6400
Charlotte Amalie, VI 00802

# Index

Page numbers in *italics* indicate illustrations.

# Meet the Author

Sylvia McNair was born in Korea and believes she inherited a love of travel from her missionary parents. She grew up in Vermont. After graduating from Oberlin College, she held a variety of jobs, married, had four children, and settled in the Chicago area. She now lives in Evanston, Illinois. She is the author of several travel guides and nearly two dozen books for young people published by Children's Press.

"This book about the territories of the United States was especially interesting to me, because I learned a lot about our nation's history and our relations with people in many parts of the world. The background, geography, and culture of the islands in the Pacific and the Caribbean are little-known but important chapters in the American story.

"When I start to write a new book, I read everything I can find about the subject: books, encyclopedia entries, magazine and newspaper articles. The Internet is another important source of information. I interview people who have a particular interest in my subject matter. When writing about a place, it always helps if I'm able to visit it. Every place has its own atmosphere and history, different from all others.

"I hope the young people who read this book will continue to find out more about these other parts of the United States scattered around the Earth. If you read books about faraway places, watch television shows about their history and geography, and ask questions of people who have been there, you can almost imagine you are actually traveling. And perhaps someday you'll see them for yourselves."

McNair has traveled in all fifty states and more than forty other countries. "Wherever I go, I find something to enjoy and appreciate."

# Photo Credits